Estonians in the *Waffen-SS*

Estonians in the *Waffen-SS*

The *20. Waffen-Grenadier-Division der SS (estnische Nr. 1)*

Rolf Michaelis

Schiffer Military History
Atglen, PA

Book Translation by David Johnston

Book Design by Stephanie Daugherty.

Library of Congress Control Number: 2009929045

Printed in China.
ISBN: 978-0-7643-3350-7
This book was originally published in German under the title
Esten in der Waffen-SS
Die 20. Waffen-Grenadier-Division der SS (estnische Nr.1)

We are interested in hearing from authors with book ideas on related topics.

Published by Schiffer Publishing Ltd.
4880 Lower Valley Road
Atglen, PA 19310
Phone: (610) 593-1777
FAX: (610) 593-2002
E-mail: Info@schifferbooks.com.
Visit our web site at: www.schifferbooks.com
Please write for a free catalog.
This book may be purchased from the publisher.
Please include $5.00 postage.
Try your bookstore first.

In Europe, Schiffer books are distributed by:
Bushwood Books
6 Marksbury Avenue
Kew Gardens
Surrey TW9 4JF, England
Phone: 44 (0) 20 8392-8585
FAX: 44 (0) 20 8392-9876
E-mail: Info@bushwoodbooks.co.uk.
Visit our website at: www.bushwoodbooks.co.uk

Table of Contents

Foreword

When the German 18th Army crossed the Estonian border on 7 July 1941 as part of "Operation Barbarossa," the approximately 1,125,000 Estonians welcomed it as a liberator from bolshevism. As the German troops advanced through the country—approximately 47,500 km^2 in area—they encountered armed freedom fighters, whom they dubbed "forest brothers." On 22 June 1941 these Estonians had begun attacking smaller Soviet units and supply lines.

In August 1941 the *Wehrmacht* began employing these Estonian rebels to form security units to guard supply lines. Simultaneously, the Order Police began recruiting in an effort to reorganize the Estonian police.

Recognizing a potential source of manpower, in summer 1942 the *Waffen-SS* formed the Estonian SS Legion, which gave rise first to the Estonian Volunteer Brigade and then the 20th Estonian SS Volunteer Division.

This work is intended to document the history of these Estonians, and will examine the previously-mentioned formations of the *Wehrmacht* and Order Police, as well as the border police units formed after general mobilization in February 1944, since the remnants of these were all incorporated into the *20. Waffen-Grenadier-Division der SS (estnische Nr. 1)* in late 1944-early 1945.

The book reveals reasons, operations, and motivations, but it cannot reflect the horror associated with military actions in time of war. The reader can appreciate that people on all sides—soldiers and civilians alike—endured great suffering and misery.

Berlin, October 2000
Rolf Michaelis

Estonia

On the original territory of Estonia (*Eesti* in Estonian), the northernmost of the Baltic States on the Gulf of Finland, an independent Estonian people emerged at the end of the 4th Century. They spoke Estonian, a Finno-Ugrioan dialect. German and Danish troops occupied the area from 1207 to 1227. In 1346 the Danes sold their portion to the Order of Teutonic Knights. There developed a Baltic-German and clerical upper class which, though it transformed several cities into thriving trading centers, viewed the Estonian population as little more than serfs.

In 1558 the entry of Russian troops under Ivan the Terrible sparked the Livonian War, and in 1561 the Swedish King Erik IV claimed Estonia as a Swedish province. Sweden also occupied southern Estonia and northern Latvia, and merged these into the Province of Livonia. The Great Northern War for mastery of the Baltic and the nations bordering it was fought from 1700 to 1721. Denmark, Saxony, Poland, and Russia, and from 1713 also Prussia and Hanover, fought against Sweden. The Peace of Nystad (1721) forced Sweden to cede Estonia and Livonia to Russia, and the Swedes lost their dominant position in the east.

Czar Nicholas I (1796 – 1855) diminished the privileges formerly enjoyed by the Baltic Germans. His successor, Czar Alexander I (1818 – 1881), went even further; on one hand abolishing serfdom, while on the other intensifying efforts to Russify the provinces attached to his empire. Czar Alexander III (1845 – 1894) made this the cornerstone of his policy, and in 1888-89 the Baltic nobility lost many privileges, for example, the right to appoint judges and policemen, and Russian became the official language.

In 1905 there were revolts, directed mainly against the Baltic-German upper class. After the Russian Revolution of 1917 the provisional Russian government granted the Estonians the right of self-determination. The administrative structure of the provinces was changed, and the Estonian province, together with the northern part of Livonia (southern Estonian), formed a self-governed area. On 24 February 1918 the Estonian National Assembly proclaimed a republic independent of Russia.[1]

As the Baltic-German gentry desired to regain its former power, it called for the occupation of the country by German forces. From 25 February to 12 November 1918 the country did in fact find itself under German military administration; however, when German forces withdrew from the Baltic States Russian troops marched back in. Fierce fighting broke out between Estonian and Russian units, with German *Freikorps* in some cases helping in the struggle against the communists. The Germans also fell upon the rear of the Estonian units, however, resulting in a battle near Wenden in which Estonian troops achieved a decisive victory over the *Freikorps*. Since then 23 June 1919 has been celebrated in Estonia as a holiday.

At the beginning of the 1930s 88% of the population was Estonian, 8.2% Russian, and 1.5% German. More than 75% of the inhabitants were Protestant.

The economy was based on the cultivation of wheat and flax, as well as cattle breeding, fishing, and the oil shale industry. The main exports were oil, wood, cellulose, and butter.

In the Hitler-Stalin Pact Germany renounced any influence in the Baltic republics and resettled the German population. This was done to escape the threat of Soviet occupation, which became fact on 21 June 1940. Stalin annexed the country on 6 August 1940 and it became part of the USSR.[2] Many Estonian leaders fled to Finland, where they constituted an Estonian liberation committee in May 1941. After the outbreak of war between Germany and the Soviet Union on 22 June 1941, it sent a note to the German foreign minister in which Dr. Massakas was named envoy of the sovereign and neutral Republic of Estonia. The German response to the request for the resumption of diplomatic relations was the arrest of Dr. Massakas.[3] Germany had no interest in granting sovereignty to Estonia or the other Baltic States.

With the rapid advance by the German forces, on 20 September 1941 Estonia became the rear area of Army Group North, commanded by *General* von Roques.[4] He gave the fascist Dr. Mäe authority to set up a pro-German administration. Prior to the Second World War Estonia had granted the Jewish segment of the population cultural autonomy, and the Estonians remained relatively liberal even after the German occupation. The situation led *SS-Brigadeführer* Stahlecker[5] to lament that his *Einsatzgruppe A* had been unable to provoke "*a single spontaneous anti-Jewish demonstration leading to a pogrom*," and that the Estonian self-defense force was arresting Jews but not liquidating them.[6]

Lithuania and Latvia had already been transferred from military administration to the Eastern Ministry on 1 September 1941. The Reich minister for the occupied eastern territories, Alfred Rosenberg, characterized the majority of Lithuanians as "*racially inferior*," and in his opinion the Latvians had been "*considerably infiltrated by Russian racial elements*." On 5 December of that year his *Reichkommissariat Ostland* also took over Estonia. Rosenberg had a somewhat higher opinion of the Estonians, calling them the "*elite of the Baltic peoples*." Hinrich Lohse, appointed *Reichkommissar Ostland*, had a more moderate view of the three nations, but this was due more to disinterest on his part than humanity. At the end of 1942, however, prompted by critical coworkers, he became more active and composed a 51-page memo for Rosenberg, in which he proposed a change in direction in Germany's policies in the *Ostland*.

Even before this, *SA-Obergruppenführer* Litzmann,[7] in his capacity as general commissar of Estonia, took up the interests of the Estonian people. He explained the Estonians' resignation after their initial joy at the end of bolshevism as follows:

> "*The dualism of our policy—we take economic measures as if we were operating in a district that is part of the Reich, while we keep the population in the dark as to their future—must by necessity create tensions and bring about the opposite of what we are striving to achieve.*"

There was a concrete shift in the policies of the Eastern Ministry when *SS-Gruppenführer* Berger[8] took over the post of state secretary and, with an eye toward recruiting Estonian volunteers, motivated Rosenberg to work out an independent status for the Baltic nations. After initial interest in turning the *Reichkommissariat Ostland* into a protectorate of the Reich, however, on 8 February 1943 Hitler rejected all desires for autonomy by the Baltic peoples. In the wrangling for German concessions the *Waffen-SS* and *Wehrmacht*, together with politicians like Litzmann and, to some degree, Rosenberg, were opposed to the ideas of Bormann and Lohse. The latter was worried most of all about his own position!

The front in Estonia collapsed in September 1944. On the 21st of the month—almost three years to the day since its capture by Germany—Soviet forces took the Estonian capital of Reval. Two days later the last German troops left the country, which became a Soviet republic for the next 44 years.

The "*Rahvarinne*" People's Front established itself on 13 April 1988, and on 16 November of that year the Supreme Soviet announced Estonia's independence. On 30 March 1990 the parliament declared the continuance of the republic established in 1918, and on 3 April elected Edgar Savissaar prime minister. On 8 May 1990 the Republic of Estonia was officially created. Lennart Meri has been president since 1997—Mart Laar became prime minister in the second electoral period.

Estonians in the Army

When German forces crossed the Estonian border in early July 1941 they immediately received support from Estonian rebels, who either assisted the Germans in their fight against the Red Army or engaged smaller Soviet units on their own. The German 18th Army, operating in the Baltic States, assembled and organized these partisan units, and in August of that year established the:

Estonian Security Battalion 181,[9] with the 1st-4th Squads (*Hundertschaften*)
Estonian Security Battalion 182 with the 5th-8th Squads
Estonian Security Battalion 183 with the 9th-12th and 17th Squads

followed in October 1941 by:

Estonian Security Battalion 184 with the 13th-16th and 18th Squads
Estonian Security Battalion 185 with the 19th-22nd Squads

and finally in spring 1942:

Estonian Security Battalion 186 with the 23rd-26th Squads

Each battalion had an authorized strength of 657 men, of which 57 served in the headquarters, and the rest in companies of 150 men each. In fact the total varied, in part because some battalions had four squads and others five.

Effective 15 May 1942 the Estonian security battalions were supposed to be incorporated into the *Ordnungspolizei* as Police Battalions 281 – 286. Following a meeting held by the commander of the *Ordnungspolizei* in Riga, however, it was decreed that Battalions 281 – 286 were to be given back to the army by 21 August 1942.

When the service obligations of the volunteers expired, the Estonian security battalions were disbanded effective 23 October 1942. As many members were unhappy about the conditions of their service, only about half of them wanted to continue in German service. These men formed new units which were dubbed *Ost-Bataillone (estnische) 658 – 660*. Their subordination to the *Wehrmacht* ended on 20 April 1944 when, with a strength of about 1,800 men, they were sent to the *20. Waffen-Grenadier-Division der SS (estnische Nr. 1)*.

Members of the Estonian Self-Defense Force.

Estonian officers of an Eastern Battalion.

Estonian and German officers of an Eastern Battalion.

Cigarette break.

Eating in an underground bunker.

Estonians in the *Wehrmacht*.

Dr. Mäe received *Major* Rebane, wearer of the Knight's Cross.

Estonians in the *Ordnungspolizei* (Order Police)

The German *Ordnungspolizei* (Order Police) had far greater opportunities and interest in using Estonian volunteers. Like the army, it took in the first volunteers in the summer. As Estonia was under military administration until 5 December 1941, until then the *Ordnungspolizei* was not tasked with prison duties, and instead had three months in which to take care of administrative tasks for its coming mission.

On 21 October 1941 the commander of the Rear Army Area North ordered a thorough organization of the volunteer units formed and yet to be formed in the rear army area. In December of that year the men attached to the *Ordnungspolizei* were designated police squads.[11] These were initially organized into battalions for anti-partisan operations[12] and police squads (O) for tasks of the police order force and (W) for tasks in the guard and security service (object protection). On 26 October 1941 responsibility for the formation of the mobile police battalions was passed to Police Battalion 321 (*Major der Schutzpolizei* Petersen) by order of the senior SS and police commander.

Within Estonia the police battalions were established in Dorpat (Tartu), Fellin (Viljandi), Pöltsamaa, and Pleskau (Pskov), and on 4 December 1941 they were given the battalion numbers 37 – 42. Each battalion had an authorized strength of 507 men and was organized into a headquarters (57 men) and three companies of 150 men each. As the situation developed, the commander of the *Ordnungspolizei* formed additional units with the agreement of the local commanders. By order of the Senior SS and Police Commander for the *Ostland* these units received the following numbers:

Police Battalion 29 in Reval (Talinn)
Police Battalion 30 in Reval
Police Battalion 31 in Wesenberg (Rakvere)
Police Battalion 32 in Werro (Vöru)
Police Battalion 33 in Dorpat
Police Battalion 34 in Werro
Police Battalion 35 in Pernau (Pärnu)
Police Battalion 36 in Arensburg (Kuressaare)

By order of the senior SS and police commander, on 3 March 1942 Police Battalion 29 moved by rail from Reval to Krasnogvardeysk. It was given postal number 46 623 and was assigned to coastal defense between Leningrad and Oranienbaum. With the end of their service agreement, on 17 November 1942 the men returned from the front to Dorpat. There volunteers were mustered out for the Estonian SS Legion for the duration of the war.

More units were required at the front, and on 29 March 1942 Police Battalion 33 was dispatched by truck to Krasnoye-Selo. It was assigned postal number 47 797, and was also tasked with coastal defense as part of Police Battle Group Jeckeln. The Estonians returned to Pernau on 4 December 1942, and once again an effort was made to recruit volunteers for the Estonian SS Legion for the duration of the war.

By order of the Commander of the *Ordnungspolizei* for the Ostland issued on 22 March 1942, in matters of personnel the reinforced Estonian border control service was subordinated to the commander of the *Ordnungspolizei*. From its members the latter established Police Battalions 43, 44, and 45 (customs).

On 1 June 1942 a decree by the *Reichsführer-SS* and Chief of German Police created the following ranks for the members of units of the *Schutzmannschaft* (police):

Schutzmann
Unterkorporal
Vizekorporal
Korporal
Vizefeldwebel
Kompaniefeldwebel
Zugführer und Leutnant der Schutzmannschaft
Oberzugführer und Oberleutnant der Schutzmannschaft
Kompanieführer und Oberleutnant der Schutzmannschaft
Bataillonsführer und Major/Oberstleutnant der Schutzmannschaft

On 29 July 1942 Police Battalion 36 received orders to undertake anti-partisan operations in White Russia. On 2 August it was sent by rail from Dorpat to Novogrodek, then on 28 August 1942 it was committed at the front in the Don Bend. Fierce defensive fighting cost the battalion 37 dead, 97 wounded, and 11 missing. The battalion returned to Reval on 4 February 1943 to be mustered out for the Estonian SS Legion.

On 1 October 1942 the commander of the *Ordnungspolizei* based in Reval had 591 German policemen, 5,110 Estonians in individual service, and 5,385 Estonians in the police battalions.

By an order of the *Reichsführer-SS* and Chief of German Police issued on 16 December 1942, the Estonian Self-Defense Force was used to create Police Battalions 287 to 293 (total strength 2,837 men).

As parts of the police units had moved over to the Estonian SS Legion, some units were given new numbers:

Police Battalion 287 became Police Battalion 29
Police Battalion 288 became Police Battalion 30
Police Battalion 289 became Police Battalion 31
Police Battalion 290 became Police Battalion 32
Police Battalion 293 became Police Battalion 33
Police Battalion 30 became Police Battalion 35

Police Battalions 291 and 292 were disbanded and their personnel distributed among Police Battalions 29 and 32. The rest of the original Battalions 29 and 33 formed the new Police Battalion 287.

Thus, there existed in Estonia on 1 April 1943 19 police battalions (29 – 45 and 287) with a combined strength of 327 officers, 1,328 NCOs, and 5,919 *Schutzmänner*. As well, there was the City Individual Police Service with 41 officers and 648 men and the Country Individual Police Service with 112 officers and 1,097 men.[13] Compared to the total strength on 1 October 1942 of 11,086 Estonians, plus the 2,837 members of the self-defense force who had joined them, the figure of 9,472 policemen represented a drop in strength. The majority of the missing 4,551 men had no motivation to remain in German service after their service contract ended. Only about 1,000 of them joined the Estonian SS Legion.

On 9 December 1943 a decree was issued ordering the Estonian *Schutzmannschaft* battalions renamed Estonian *Polizei* battalions. Three months later the following units were issued postal numbers when they were ordered to the front to defend their homeland:

Estonian Police Battalion 29	04 826
Estonian Police Battalion 30	07 002
Estonian Police Battalion 31	05 499

On 4 May 1944 Estonian Police Regiment 1 was formed (postal no. 13 036). It was disbanded four months later. Other units received postal numbers on 21 June 1944:

Estonian Police Battalion 34	43 326
Estonian Police Battalion 37	45 380
Estonian Police Battalion 38	46 903
Estonian Police Battalion 40	44 721
Estonian Police Replacement Battalion 41	44 445
Estonian Police Replacement Battalion 42	43 167

Most of the Estonian police battalions were disbanded by September 1944, with only a few surviving until January 1945. These included Police Battalions 35 and 37 to 39, which took part in the defensive fighting from Dorpat to Riga and helped defend the Latvian capital for a week. In the evacuation of Estonia they came to Germany, where in the winter of 1944-45 they were attached to the *20. Waffen-Grenadier-Division der SS (estnische Nr. 1)*. The rest remained in the country and fell into Soviet hands.

Leaving for the front.

The commander of the Order Police inspects Police Battalion 29 after its return from action at the front.

Training on the heavy machine-gun.

Marchpast by Police Battalion 36 in Dorpat.

Police Battalion 33 marches out of garrison, bound for the front.

Estonians in the SS[14] Border Police Regiments

After Dr. Mäe, director of the Estonian self-administration, ordered compulsory military service on 30 January 1944, *SS-Oberführer* Soodla, the Inspector-General of the Estonian SS Legion, began calling up the draftees.[15] Four days later the Senior SS and Police Commander Russia-North announced the formation of three border police regiments. Although the draftees were often highly motivated out of fear and hatred of the Red Army, this soon dropped sharply because of inadequate organization, weapons, and equipment, as well as poor training. The potential effectiveness of the units was thus questionable from the start.

Most of the Estonian border police regiments were attached to the 300th Special Purpose Division[16] and the 207th Security Division along Lake Peipus. The following is from the history of the latter division:

"After the division of Grenadier Regiment 374, the 94th Security Regiment was the most capable element of the division. Reinforced by artillery and anti-aircraft guns, it was deployed to defend the island of Piirissar. The remaining lake front was held mainly by Estonian regiments. Even in the spring, establishing and training these units represented a significant portion of the division's responsibilities. Each Estonian regiment had a German liaison detachment with a German officer, to whom reported a German Feldwebel attached to each battalion and a Gefreite attached to each company. In turn the Estonians assigned a liaison officer to division headquarters in the form of Captain Jaakson, with whom there was an excellent working relationship.

Some of the Estonian officers came from the Estonian police battalions, some from anti-partisan groups, and most had served actively in the Estonian or Russian army. Most were well-intentioned but lacked ability, simply let things take their course, and tended to abuse alcohol. Their behavior could be explained by growing doubts about prospects of a German victory and the disillusionment they had experienced at German hands concerning their national independence. Nevertheless, an inspection of Estonian units by the Commander-in-Chief of Army Group North, Generaloberst Model, came off not too badly."

Concerning the motivation of the Estonian members of the SS Border Police units, Army Detachment Narva reported on 18 August 1944:

"The 207th Security Division, lacking any significant fighting strength, was pushed together on the right. The Estonians in the division have given up, fleeing into the woods or going home…"

On 3 September 1944, while accompanying the commander of the 207th Security Division on a visit to the Estonian 5th SS Border Police Regiment, which was deployed on both sides of the road, *Major* Dr. von Below had the following experience:

"*...the Estonians came towards us in a mass across the width of the road. The commanding officer, the driver and I tried to halt the Estonians, first with words then with drawn pistols. Finally we forced them to go to ground facing in the direction of the enemy. We expected the Russians to attack from over the next rise at any moment. But nothing happened, and the Estonian regimental commander was furious when we reached him and advised him that his unit had abandoned him.*"

According to statements by former members, the elements of the six SS border police regiments captured by the Soviets were often simply integrated into the Red Army and immediately used against German troops in Estonia. Other elements under German control were sent back to Germany, to the area of Gotenhafen. About this the war diary of the 4*th* SS Volunteer Panzer-Grenadier Brigade *Nederland* noted on 22 September 1944:

"*An Estonian replacement battalion approaching Pernau. Estonian Replacement Regiment Fellin nearing Pernau from the SW, last elements about 25 km SE of Pernau at about 1400 hours. Despite a vehicle shortage, the brigade provided 30 tons of transport space to get them out quickly, as both units were supposed to be put aboard ships for Germany.*"

In the Gotenhafen area the Estonian SS Border Police Training and Replacement Regiment set up a collection point for the rest of the various evacuated units. In mid-October the SS Border Police units in Germany were ordered to Neuhammer for integration into the *20. Waffen-Grenadier-Division der SS (estnische Nr. 1).*

Estonians in the *Waffen-SS*

As a consequence of its desire for a sovereign Estonia, the Estonian administration permitted by the Germans also developed plans in the military sphere. In 1941-42 the former department head in the General Staff of the Republic of Estonia, Colonel Soodla,[17] together with senior Estonian officers, composed a memorandum that was handed over to the German authorities. Its objective was to again form armed forces under Estonian command. The Estonian volunteers serving in the *Wehrmacht* and the *Ordnungspolizei* would form the core of these forces. The General Commissar of Estonia, *SA-Obergruppenführer* Litzmann,[18] promised to support the idea.

At the same time, on 21 May 1942 *SS-Sturmbannführer* With, working in the staff of the Senior SS and Police Commander Russia-North, put to paper a memorandum in which he made reference to potential Baltic volunteers for the *Waffen-SS*. The *Reichsführer-SS* initially rejected the idea, however:

"The formation of Waffen-SS units of Estonians, Latvians or Lithuanians is certainly tempting, but inherently very dangerous."

The first step had been taken, however, and Himmler's belief that Estonia had supposedly been "Germanized" over the centuries led him to approach Hitler with the idea of forming a unit of the *Waffen-SS* in Estonia. As in the Scandinavian countries, there were many so-called "Nordic-looking people"[19] there, especially in the northwest. Finally, on 1 October 1942, Hitler authorized the formation of an Estonian SS legion.[20] This was his response to the Estonian desire for armed forces under their own command and was primarily a propaganda exercise. Of course, the knowledge of the volunteers' unsuitability in the *Wehrmacht* and *Ordnungspolizei* was decisive. With the one-year service contracts about to expire, it was predictable that few of the Estonians would choose to continue serving in the existing formations. Of the approximately 4,500 Estonians whose periods of service were ending, only about 1,000 chose to join the Estonian SS Legion. These came almost exclusively from Police Battalions 29, 33, and 36, whose year of service ran out in September 1942. The first 113 members departed Tallinn (Reval) for the SS training camp at Debica on 8 October 1942, and five days later, after passing through Latvia and East Prussia, they arrived at the heath camp (Heidelager) in the General Government.

SS-Untersturmführer Maitla,[21] leader of the first transport, initially established two companies under the command of *SS-Untersturmführer* Pirk and *SS-Standartenjunker* Kompus. At the end of October 1942 the legion was bolstered by the arrival of four *SS-Standartenoberjunker* from the SS officer cadet school in Brunswick. More Estonians and additional German core personnel arrived soon afterwards.[22] 80 officers of the former Estonian Army were sent to the SS officer cadet school in Tölz and 60 former NCOs to the SS non-commissioned officer school in Posen.

In November 1942 the legion was organized into three grenadier companies and a heavy company with mortars and heavy machine-guns. An anti-tank company was also formed under the command of *SS-Untersturmführer* Langhorst.[23] The legion's ultimate planned organization was:

Legion Headquarters with Headquarters Company
I Battalion (1st – 4th Companies)
II Battalion (5th – 8th Companies)
III Battalion (9th – 12th Companies)
Infantry Gun Company
Anti-Tank Company
Pioneer Company

Instead of the *Sig-Runen*, the Estonians were initially issued plain black collar patches with no insignia.[24] Later the men also wore the Estonian national colors in the form of a badge on the left (in some cases also on the right) sleeve. Some who came from the *Wehrmacht* or police squads continued wearing the sleeve insignia used there, three lions on a blue-black-white badge.

After the necessary vehicles had been delivered to the Legion the training of mechanics and drivers began. This enabled the Legion's I Battalion (*SS-Hauptsturmführer* Eberhard) to become fully motorized. At the end of November 1942 *SS-Obersturmbannführer* Augsberger,[25] the designated commanding officer, and 147 members of the SS *Totenkopf* Infantry Replacement Battalion III from Brünn reached the Legion. Training had initially followed the Estonian pattern because of a shortage of German instructors, but now German methods were introduced.

At the end of January 1943 the first Estonians returned to the Legion from the SS NCO school in Posen. At the same time another 75 members of the unit left for training at the SS NCO school in Lauenburg. On 21 January 1943 two officers, 24 NCOs, and 62 enlisted men arrived from the disbanded 1st Company of the SS Special Purpose Battalion to serve as German core personnel.[26]

Relationships between the German core personnel and the Estonians varied. While, for example, *SS-Obersturmführer* Lessing, adjutant of the later *Waffen-Grenadier-Regiment der SS 45*, characterized the Estonians as "swine" and was sent to the *600. Infanterie-Division (russische Nr. 1)* as a result, or *SS-Hauptsturmführer* Wallner (commander of the 20th SS Fusilier Battalion), who labeled Riipalu as "just an Estonian" and was subsequently transferred to a Ukrainian unit, there were also German officers and NCOs who were highly respected by the Estonians; for example, *SS-Sturmbannführer* Eberhardt (commander of SS Panzer-Grenadier Battalion *Narwa*), *SS-Obersturmführer* Schmidt (*SS-Sturmbannführer* Eberhardt's adjutant), and *SS-Obersturmführer* Laumann (SS Panzer-Grenadier Battalion *Narwa*'s medical officer).

In spring 1943, based on a decree by the Reich Minister for the Occupied Eastern Territories concerning the obligation to perform labor service dated 19 December 1941, orders were issued for the call-up of the entire Estonian male population from the year classes 1919-1924, as well as all older officers and NCOs of the former national armed forces not yet in service. In November 1943 the call-up was extended to include year classes 1915 and up. In hand with this the Legion's training and replacement battalion was established on 22 February 1943.[27] Dr. Hjalmar Mäe recalled:

"The draftees had to undress in front of the committee for medical examination. Before they were allowed to dress again they had to decide if they wanted to voluntarily join the Estonian Legion of the Waffen-SS and sign a declaration to that effect. If they didn't, they were either sent to the front to serve as auxiliaries for Army Group North or to Germany to work as forced laborers in the armaments industry, depending on the decision of the committee."

By the end of March 1943 the Estonian SS Legion achieved battalion strength:

Officers	NCOs	Enlisted Men	Total
37	175	757	969
3.8%	18%	78.2%	100%

The later *Waffen-Unterscharführer* Leinhard Miländer joined the *Waffen-SS* as a sixteen-year-old:

"I was born in the Pärnu district on 21 August 1926 and completed the 6 classes of the Progynmasium. At 16 I was too young for the police or the Wehrmacht's eastern battalions, so I volunteered for the Estonian SS Legion, about which I had learned from a recruiting poster. My parents signed an authorization form and I went by train to Tallinn, to the recruiting station there. My main motivation was the struggle against communism.

After a few days I was sent to Debica. Trained as a machine-gunner, in October 1943 I accompanied the brigade by train to Idritsa – Nevel and saw frontline action there."

Alexander Zahharov was assigned to the Estonian SS Legion from the *Ordnungspolizei*:

"I came into the world on 26 October 1916, the son of a Russian officer and a German mother. As a result of the Hitler-Stalin pact, while working for a trust company I was suddenly arrested and quickly deported from Estonian as an ethnic-German! At first I lived in a refugee camp in Mainfranken and in July 1941 I reported for military service with other ethnic Germans. They promised us that we would be sent to Estonia to fight elements of the Red Army left there. In August 1941 I joined the Ostland Police Battalion in Frankfurt/Oder.

Things turned out very differently and instead of Estonia, in October 1941 I was sent to the 5th Police District in Kiev, where I remained until July 1942. In October 1942 they transferred me to the Estonian SS Legion in Debica. I had nothing to do with the transfer; no one had asked me if I wanted to go! There I was made a Legion-Rottenführer, which was equivalent to my previous rank.

At the training camp there was a big brawl between German and Estonian soldiers, in which the mess was completely wrecked. Otherwise the two sides got along well."

Leo Sipelgas described the training period at the Heidelager SS Training Camp:

"I was born in Pärnu on 14 January 1926, the son of an Estonian and a Baltic-German mother and on 23 April 1943 I joined the Estonian SS Legion as a 17-year-old. Besides my lust for adventure, hatred of the Russians was my main motivation—the Soviets had sent my parents to Siberia. My father died in 1940, my mother in 1949.

The SS training camp at Heidelager was a former training camp for Polish cavalry and consisted of four so-called rings. We were in the 4th ring. Around each ring were six-man barracks and two so-called mess barracks. Inside the ring was the parade square and two vehicle garages.

During our time there the training camp, about 20 hectares in size, was guarded by Rumanians—as well, in the 3rd ring were members of the Galician SS Volunteer Division. In addition to Polish civilian personnel (barbers, shoemakers, photographers and even a brothel aptly named Waldeslust, run by a 50-year-old lady from Hamburg), there was a small work camp at the Kochanowka railway station, where Jews and Poles were imprisoned. The Jewish men, who all wore the Star of David, maintained the roads, took away the garbage, cleaned the toilets and were forced to do many other dirty jobs. After about four months, however, they all went away. The families of the officers were housed outside the heath camp.

The daily routine was wakeup at 0600, breakfast at 0630, drill from 0700 to 1145. Lunch was from 1200 to 1230, followed by rest until 1300. Then there was political instruction until 1400 and from 1400 to 1500 we were often at the outdoor firing range. We trained in the field until 1700 and after cleaning our weapons we usually went off duty. Night exercises were scheduled twice a week. The training was already quite tough.

From Heidelager, at the end of June 1943 I went to the SS Interpreter School in Oranienburg and from there to Metz for artillery training."

Heidelager training camp.

Marching to the swearing-in ceremony at Heidelager, autumn 1942.

Inspection of the Estonian SS Legion in Debica. In the center is *SS-Standartenführer* Augsberger.

Commanding officer *SS-Standartenführer* Augsberger addresses the men, autumn 1942.

Marching back to quarters. Note the right collar patch without runes and the ribbon of the Eastern Peoples Decoration in the second buttonhole of the *Legion-Untersturmführer* on the right of the photo.

German and Estonian non-commissioned officers, autumn 1942.

Still full of confidence...

SS-Standartenführer Augsberger

Variations of the collar patch.

Variations of the sleeve badge.

Armband worn by a unit of the self-defense force.

SS Panzergrenadier-Bataillon Narwa

(March 1943 – March 1944)

After I Battalion of the Estonian SS Legion was sworn in on 13 February 1943, on 23 March the SS-FHA attached the 975-man-strong unit to the *SS-Panzergrenadier-Division Wiking* stationed in the Ukraine.[29] This aroused displeasure among the Estonians, as they were being deployed far from their homeland. At the beginning of April 1943 the battalion arrived by train in the Lozovaya area and took over a large quantity of weapons, vehicles, and equipment from the Finnish battalion, which was returning home. For supply purposes, the unit was attached to the *SS-Panzergrenadier-Regiment Westland*.

At the end of April one officer, six non-commissioned officers, and 50 enlisted men came to the battalion from Hilvershum, forming an anti-tank platoon. At the same time 30 men were attached to the *Wiking* Division's artillery regiment and 50 to its reconnaissance battalion. On 20 May 1943 all the companies, which until then had been quartered in various villages, were assembled in Yasnaya Gorka, near Slavyansk. Strenuous combat exercises were carried out in the hot Ukrainian summer sun, but the companies were able to go to the soldiers' cinema in Slavyansk or the front theater in Kramatorsk. At the end of June 1943 a three-day battle exercise was conducted before the commanding officer of the *SS-Panzergrenadier-Division Wiking*.

Together with the rest of the *SS-Panzergrenadier-Division Wiking*, in early July 1943 the Estonians moved to a position near Belgorod, and soon afterwards the division force-marched south through Kharkov. On 18 July, after the start of the Soviet summer offensive,[30] it moved up to Andreyevka and relieved elements of the 46th Infantry Division on Hill 186.9 near Izyum. Walter Valtin, a former member of the brigade, recalled:

"I was born in Puiatus, in the Fellin District of Estonia, on 22 March 1925. Because of the general situation in Estonia after the Soviet occupation, in which members of my family were taken away, I joined the `struggle against bolshevism'.

On 15 September 1942 I was called up by the Estonian SS Legion in Viljandi (Fellin). My training began at the SS training camp in Debica near Cracow on 15 October and on 4 April 1943 I arrived in the Ukraine with the SS-Panzergrenadier-Bataillon Narwa. Most of our equipment and weapons were brand new. Each squad even had two MG 34s, later two MG 42s. Our relations with the German core personnel were proper and correct, but only seldom warm.

Things got serious for us on 18 July 1942. All was relatively quiet until about 10 AM, when a group of 22 Soviet tanks appeared. Although the order had been given to let the tanks through, one was blown up by a magnetic mine. This caused the others to change direction, placing them right in front of the muzzles of our anti-tank platoon's three 76.2-mm (Russian) and three 50-mm anti-tank guns. What followed was like an exercise on the gunnery range. Almost every second shot was a direct hit and soon the ground was littered with burning, destroyed or crippled tanks. The last three of the Soviet tanks tried to escape by backing away, however two were blown up with magnetic mines as they crossed the trenches. Only one escaped!

Two hours later Soviet artillery began pounding our battalion's positions, after which enemy tanks attacked again, this time with mounted infantry. By then additional Wehrmacht anti-tank guns had moved into position and these knocked out seven enemy tanks. We destroyed another nine in this second action, two of them by Freiwilligen-Sturmmann Heinrich Raiend singlehanded.

When the hot summer day finally came to an end, we were at last able to breathe a little easier. They were finally able to deliver water to the thirsty soldiers at the front—we missed cold water more than food. None of us got any rest during the night, as night bombers were constantly over the lines, dropping flares and fragmentation bombs. At first light we sighted about 50 enemy tanks line up as if on parade. In the ensuing attack the Red Army troops succeeded in breaking into our main line of resistance in several places. With support from Stukas and Heinkel bombers we were able to restore the line.

Our battalion commander, SS-Sturmbannführer Eberhardt, was killed on the third day of fighting. The news of his death so angered us that we counterattacked with fury and drove back the enemy, who had broken into our lines again.

During the night we were relieved by a regiment from the 42nd Infantry Division."

At the beginning of August 1943 the battalion was reformed using men returning from leave and replacements. Then, on the 12th of the month, it made an unsuccessful attack on Klenovoye, near Kharkov, under its new commander, *SS-Hauptsturmführer* Grafhorst. There followed fierce defensive fighting between Merefa and Valki, in which the battalion had to be relieved by the SS Pioneer Battalion *Wiking*. Combat strengths at that time were:

1st Company	47 men
2nd Company	35 men
3rd Company	21 men
4th Company	54 men

The men were given five days rest about 30 km behind the front, and 127 Estonians arrived from Debica as reinforcements. Following the death of *SS-Hauptsturmführer* Grafhorst on 30 August, *SS-Sturmbannführer* Oeck from the *Wiking* Division's anti-tank battalion arrived to take command of the battalion.

On 27 September the Estonians withdrew across the Dniepr and occupied a new defensive position at the mouth of the Olshana River. In early October 1943 the *SS-Panzergrenadier-Bataillon Narwa* saw action against partisans and regular enemy troops that had broken through in the Yelizavetovka and Lozovoki areas. During this relatively quiet period, the battalion received additional replacements from Debica. *Freiwilligen-Rottenführer* Alexander Zahharov was a medic during the rail transport:

"Just before Christmas a replacement transport was put together at the front near Cherkassy for the SS-Panzergrenadier-Bataillon Narwa. I was ordered to accompany the replacements as a medic and in fact was supposed to return to Debica the next day. That would have meant spending Christmas Eve in a lonely hut, and so I went up to the frontline positions to join my comrades, who welcomed me warmly.

Soon afterwards I began feeling unwell and a doctor diagnosed a severe case of neuritis. I was heading back toward the west on a hospital train, when suddenly there was shooting and explosions all around. I feared a partisan ambush—in fact, however, it turned out that it was New Year's and the men were loosing off a regular barrage to celebrate.

Finally I arrived at the Waffen-SS rest home in the Riesen Mountains and later I returned to the replacement unit in Estonia."

On 9 January 1944 the Estonians took over new positions in the forests near Irdyn, where they took part in a counterattack with Wallonian volunteers. On 25 January 1944, after a heavy artillery barrage, the Red Army breached the front at the seam between XXXXVII Army Corps[31] and XI Army Corps.[32] When enemy forces also broke through at the seam with the 4th Panzer Army (XXXXII Army Corps), it became apparent that the XI and XXXXII Army Corps were about to be encircled. On 28 January 1945 the Soviet 5th Guards Tank Army and the 6th Tank Army linked up near Zvenigorodka, trapping the two corps.[33] Hitler initially forbade a breakout from the approximately 250-kilometer-long pocket—under no circumstances was the Dniepr to be given up. Army Group South subsequently instructed the trapped units to ready powerful forces for a breakout to the south, where they would reach the German main line of resistance. The III and XXXVII Panzer Corps were supposed to advance toward the trapped units from there.

On 30 January 1944 the *SS-Panzergrenadier-Bataillon Narwa* was ordered to immediately move to Olshana and defend the town against the enemy, which had selected it as a focal point of their attack, together with the 3rd Company of the 5th SS Armored Pioneer Battalion and elements of the 5th SS Panzer Regiment. After the battle there *SS-Obersturmführer* Hein, the commander of 2nd Company, 5th SS Panzer Regiment, was decorated with the Knight's Cross. He recalled of this joint action with the Estonian volunteers:

"The 1st Company of the Narwa Battalion arrived at 1300 hours on 30 January 1944. Together with the company commander a counterattack was planned and a patrol sent out to determine how to proceed. (Company commander: SS-Untersturmführer Uhlenbusch).

Exploiting the element of surprise, the counterattack by two assault guns with mounted infantry toward Yukhovka and against Tolstaya was carried through a depression offering concealment.

Taken completely by surprise, the enemy were gripped by panic. They had taken the sound of our motors for their own tanks. The entire anti-tank line, about 6 or 7 heavy guns, was overrun and the horse-drawn limbers scattered in all directions. Two enemy tanks approached but were knocked out. The Narwa grenadiers brought in approximately 200 prisoners. The attack thus prevented the encirclement of the town of Olshana and the splitting of the pocket along the Olshana—Goroditsche road, the only paved one."

Walter Valtin recalled:

"We rested in Teklino for several days. There it was announced that we were in a pocket. No one got too upset about this, as we had faith in our own strength and command.

A little later we were moved to Olshana. In the center [of town] stood a sugar mill surrounded by high walls. Several hundred Ukrainian civilians had hidden themselves in the building's large cellars. Among them were a few partisans, who later fired at us from behind..."

The relief attempt by III Panzer Corps began on 4 February. It had to be called off after 10 days on account of bad weather, exhaustion, and failures of supply. Hitler now declared that he was ready to abandon the Dniepr. The trapped soldiers initiated the breakout at 2300 hours on 16 February 1944. The *SS-Panzergrenadier-Bataillon Narwa* formed the spearhead of the attack's left wing and forced the first breach in the encircling ring. The infantry marched through a stormy night with no heavy weapons. Enemy tanks and artillery opened fire on the soldiers, unleashing apocalyptic scenes. In their desperation the troops, some unarmed, charged the Soviet lines. Of the approximately 56,000 trapped soldiers, only about 35,000 reached III Panzer Corps the next day. This figure included 2,188 wounded who had been evacuated. Walter Valtin described the breakout:

"Everything that might hinder our progress or was unnecessary was left behind. All that we took was weapons, pouches full of ammunition and grenades. With entrenching tools and bayonets we overran several Soviet positions, then in the morning we heard the sound of heavy fighting to our right.

Suddenly German Army soldiers—possibly members of the 72nd Infantry Division—drove into the battle groups with numerous vehicles and horses and tore them apart. All mutual contact was lost. The issuing of orders and planned actions were no longer possible. The chaos became complete when Soviet tanks and artillery began firing into the moving mass. Everyone sought a way out using his own means."

After the breakout the *SS-Panzergrenadier-Bataillon Narwa* was removed from the *SS-Division Wiking* and initially transported into the Lublin area. In March 1944 the Estonian volunteers marched back to Estonia, and as part of the establishment of the 20th Estonian SS Volunteer Division formed the 20th SS Fusilier Battalion.

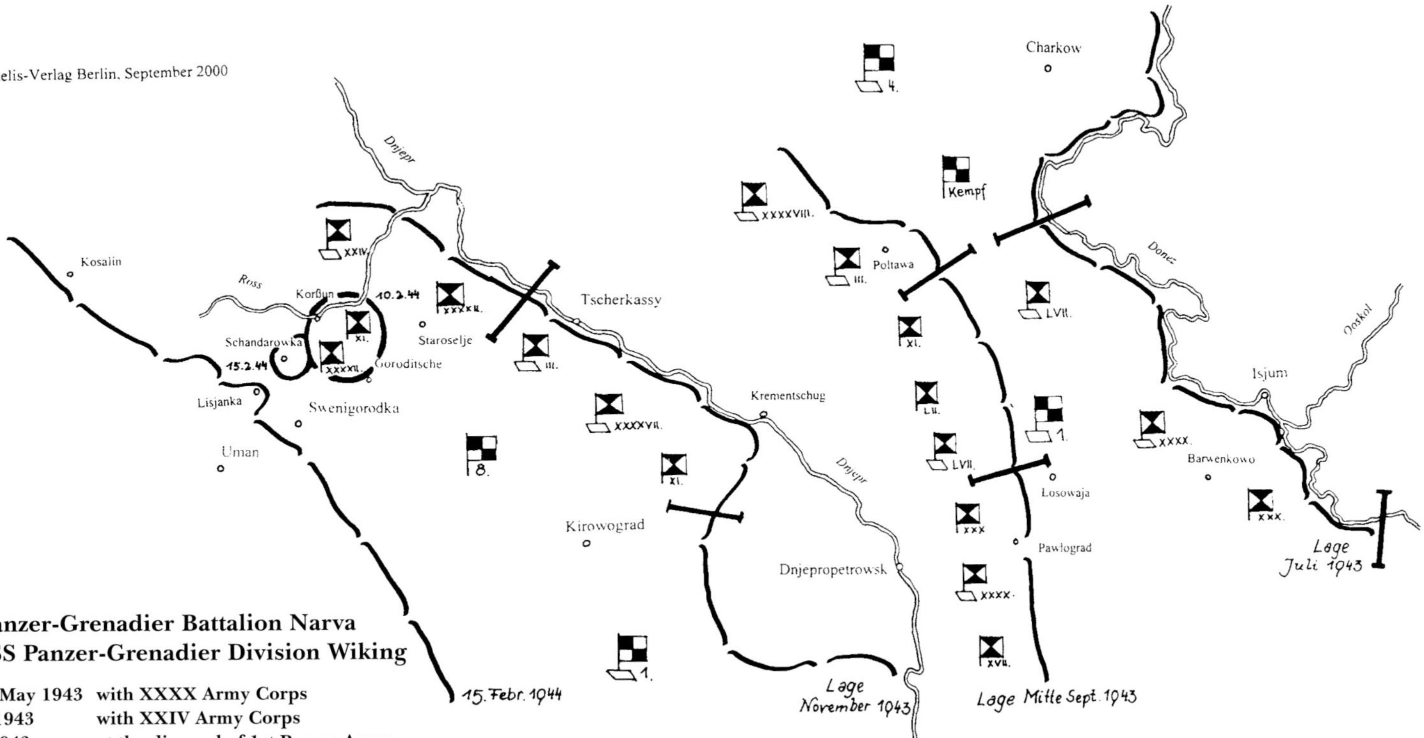

SS Panzer-Grenadier Battalion Narva with the SS Panzer-Grenadier Division Wiking

April-May 1943	with XXXX Army Corps
June 1943	with XXIV Army Corps
July 1943	at the disposal of 1st Panzer Army
August 1943	with XXXX Army Corps
Sept.-Dec. 1943	with III Panzer Corps
January 1944	with XI Army Corps
February 1944	with XXXXII Army Corps

Members of SS Panzer-Grenadier Battalion Narva.

From l. to r.: Oskar Ruut, Väino Pärtel, Hando Ruus.

Headstone for *Waffen-Hauptsturmführer* Hando Ruus in the forest cemetery in Tallinn.

The Estonian Freiwilligen-*Hauptsturmführer* Hando Ruus, the only Estonian to be awarded the German Cross in Gold.

Hando Ruus and Oskar Ruut.

SS Panzer-Grenadier Battalion Narva returned to Estonia, March 1944.

Members of
SS Panzer-Grenadier
Battalion Narva.

Destroyed materiel.

SS-Hauptsturmführer Heder, commander of the 2nd Company, SS Panzer-Grenadier Battalion Narva.

Members of the battalion.

Alexander Zahharov, seen here as a member of the 5th Police Squad in Kiev in the summer of 1942.

Walter Valtin.

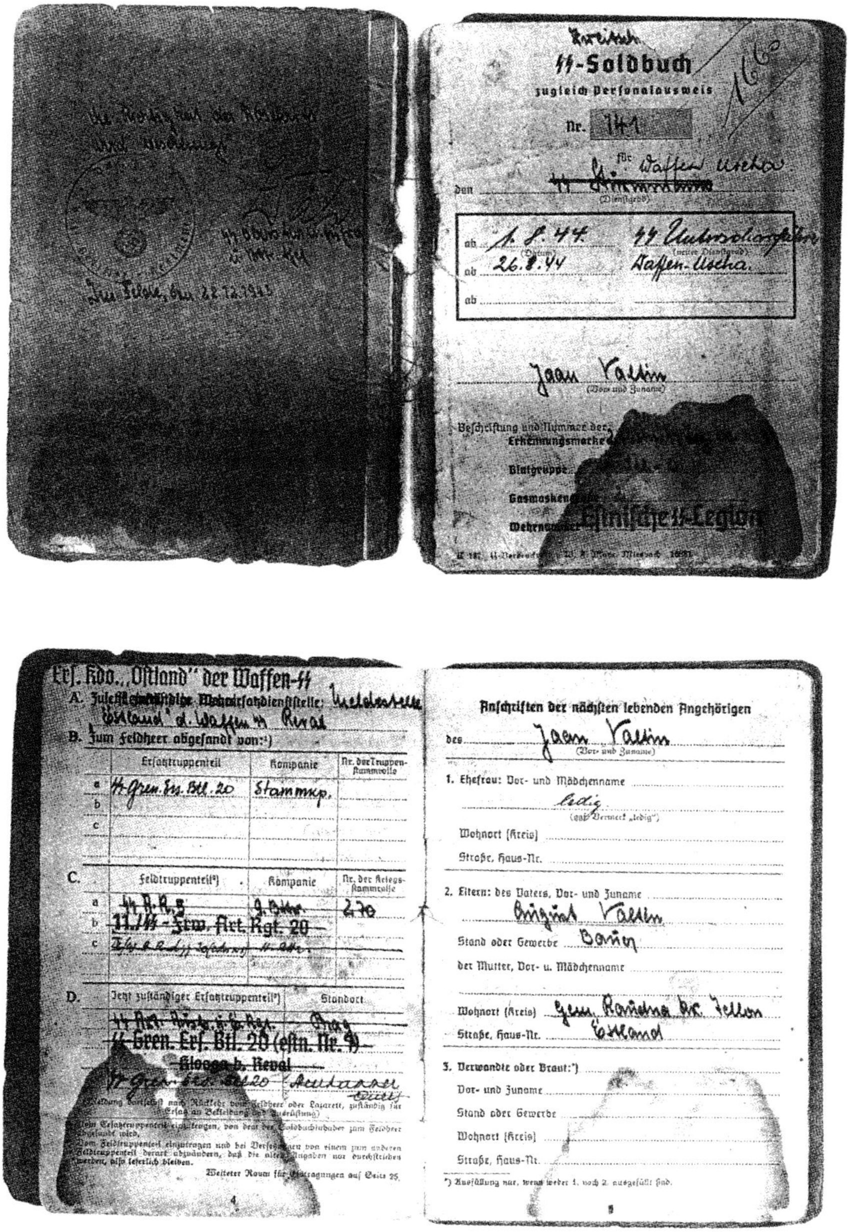

Walter Valtin's paybook.

The 3rd Estonian SS Volunteer Brigade

In March 1943 the SS-FHA planned to bring the Estonian SS Legion to brigade strength using additional recruited volunteers. After the I Battalion had been transferred to the Ukraine, formation of the 1st Estonian SS Volunteer Regiment began at the Heidelager training camp under the command of *Legion-Oberführer* Soodla.[34] As well, the 1st SS Infantry Brigade (Motorized) was to be reorganized without delay and renamed the Estonian SS Volunteer Brigade (Motorized). In addition, the 2nd Estonian SS Volunteer Regiment was to be formed at the Heidelager camp, near Debica, to complete the paying off of the 8th and 10th SS Grenadier Regiments. To accelerate the reformation process 300 members of the 1st SS Infantry Brigade (Motorized)[35] were assigned to the brigade as instructors.[36] With the formation of the brigade units the formation consisted of:

1st SS Volunteer Grenadier Regiment
2nd SS Volunteer Grenadier Regiment
SS Anti-Tank Battalion
SS Artillery Battalion
SS Flak Battalion
SS Signals Company
SS Field Replacement Battalion

After the achievement of operational readiness, in September of that year *Reichsführer-SS* Himmler inspected the Estonian volunteers at Debica training camp. Former *Freiwilligen-Unterscharführer* Leo Sipelgas recalled:

"In mid-September 1943 Himmler came to Debica for two and a half days to inspect our brigade. When he reviewed us—the headquarters company—I was standing in the front rank, as I spoke German. At the time it was a very grand feeling to be able to see the Reichsführer-SS close up—we didn't know any better… He stopped in front of us, smiled, and said: I can be proud of such soldiers! Then he moved on with Augsberger and Kurg. On the second day of the review the entire brigade marched past Himmler. He also spoke with us during a shared meal from the field kitchen, asking if we wanted to go to the front, etc. Our officers later told us that he had been very satisfied with the brigade!"

When, on 22 October 1943, the units of the *Waffen-SS* were numbered, the formation became the

3rd Estonian SS Volunteer Brigade

The two grenadier regiments initially received the numbers 42 and 43, while the brigade units were identified by the number 53. At the end of October 1943 the 3rd Estonian SS Volunteer Brigade was transported by rail to Army Group North, and there placed under the command of the Commanding General of Security Forces and Commander of Army Area North. From Riga, at the beginning of November 1943 it took part in "Operation Heinrich." Its objective was to crush the partisan republic in the Polotsk – Krasnopolye – Pustoshka – Idritsa – Sebesh area. Two battle groups were formed for the operation:

- Police Battle Group[37] Jeckeln[38]
- Police Battle Group von Gottberg[39]

The 3rd Estonian SS Volunteer Brigade was placed under the direct command of the commander of anti-partisan units, *SS-Obergruppenführer und General der Polizei* von dem Bach.[40] The assembly of units in the area south of the Sebesh—Idritsa—Pustoshka rail line for Police Battle Group Jeckeln was completed on 31 October 1943. The operation began on 1 November. For five days the partisans were attacked in the wooded area around Rosony, and the 3rd Estonian SS Volunteer Brigade advanced into the heart of the partisan republic of Albrechtovo. On 6 November the order was given to attack east in the direction of Nesherda Lake. The commander of the 42nd SS Volunteer Regiment, *Freiwilligen-Standartenführer* Kurg, was gravely wounded when his vehicle drove over a mine on the road between Idritsa and Sebesh. He died a few days later. His successor was *Freiwilligen-Sturmbannführer* Vent.[41] *Waffen-Unterscharführer* Leo Sipelgas recalled:

"About the fighting with the partisans in the Rosony area, I remember that we captured a large partisan camp. At the cost of five of our own killed, we took 20 prisoners and captured 10 horses, several peasant carts, many pigs, cows, a few kegs of vodka, tobacco, a radio station, a hospital and a printing press. In the latter we discovered thousands of newspapers plus a quantity of German-Russian dictionaries. We also discovered sacks of rubles.

During the fighting many partisans fled into the surrounding forests, and yet it was the first time I saw that many dead. We captured several Russians naked in a sauna!

Our morale was sky-high—it was our first victory and everyone wanted to charge ahead. We were all young lads and thought that victory was waiting for us…!"

As powerful Soviet units were breaching the nearby front at the same time, the operation was terminated prematurely and the units deployed to bolster the main line of resistance.[42] On 10 November 1943 von dem Bach attached the 3rd Estonian SS Volunteer Brigade to Police Battle Group Jeckeln. The next day the Estonian volunteers encountered regular Red Army troops in the area between Lakes Meshno and Nesherda.[43] Fighting began immediately, and the Estonians succeeded in halting the enemy's advance. Finally, they occupied positions from the center of Lake Nesherda to the Drissa River. On 12 November 1943, as a result of enlarging the older divisions of the *Waffen-SS* by individual regiments, the two SS volunteer grenadier regiments were renumbered from 42/43 to 45/46.

One week later Headquarters, VIII Army Corps assumed unified command of the police battle group commanded by *SS-Obergruppenführer und General der Polizei* Jeckeln and that of *Generalleutnant* Thumm in the Pustoshka – Idritsa area. The gap between the army groups created by the enemy advance posed an immense threat to the entire Eastern Front. The OKH therefore ordered the army command to seal the breach in the front immediately. First, however, the Soviet 3rd Shock Army had to be defeated near Pustoshka, and Police Battle Group Jeckeln was among the units committed. The attack was not a success and was halted on 8 December 1943. The German units pulled back to reestablish a continuous front. When the fighting died down, the soldiers began setting up quarters in which they could pass the winter.

On 16 December 1943 the 2nd Baltic Front launched an attack from the south against the so-called "Lynx Position,"[44] which ran from west to east. The Soviets soon withdrew forces from there, however, to reinforce the 1st Baltic Front, which had overrun Army Group Center's left wing, seizing an area 80 km wide and 30 km deep. Army Group North subsequently sent the 132nd Infantry Division (*Generalmajor* Wagner) to its right wing. Numerous scratch units were attached to the division, including the 3rd Estonian SS Volunteer Brigade.

On 17 December *General der Infanterie* Hoehne,[45] commanding general of the VIII Army Corps, visited the brigade and declared that the Estonians had made a good impression on him and were well-equipped. On 31 December 1943 the brigade reported its strength as:

Officers	NCOs	Enlisted Men	Total
178	864	4,057	5,099
3.5%	17%	79.5%	100%

This reveals a very balanced numerical relationship between the officers, non-commissioned officers, and enlisted men. The brigade's equipment and previous experience gained as a police battalion meant that it was deemed operational.

In the new year a large group of partisans tried unsuccessfully to break through the German lines to the east to link up with the Red Army. The partisans were confronted in battle, but they were able to slip back into the forest. On 31 January 1944 Headquarters, I Army Corps, which was taking over the area, noted in a memo to Headquarters, 16th Army:[46]

"*For command and supply reasons, at least two, if not three, division headquarters must be deployed in the sector between the marshy area south of the Drissa and the left corps boundary. The departure of Headquarters, 290th Infantry Division with its supply units will cause a further worsening of the situation, which can be made good temporarily because the Estonian Brigade is directly attached to the corps as an independent command staff, while the 132nd Infantry Division must command from mid Lake Nesherda to the left corps boundary. This situation appears untenable in the long run, therefore it is requested that a division with signals resources and sufficient anti-tank weapons be sent at a later date.*"

In February 1944 the SS war correspondent Berend von Rottbeck wrote a typical propaganda report on the actions of the 3rd Estonian SS Volunteer Brigade for the paper "*Reiter 'gen Osten*":

"*The Estonian SS Volunteer Brigade has been in action for several weeks. In that time its men have received their baptism of fire and gained their first frontline experience. They have gotten to know the land that is their battleground: the loneliness of the endless forests, the quiet, impassible moors and swamps. They have marched along the roads, whose viscous mud seems to make any forward progress impossible but which in reality is no more of an obstacle than the attacks by Bolshevik bandits...*

When the brigade arrived in its assigned area of operations, it was initially given the task of clearing it of Bolshevik bandits in cooperation with other units. First contact with the enemy occurred on the second day of the advance. Previously the retreating Bolshevik bandits had offered no resistance, limiting themselves instead to complicating and delaying the unit's advance by mining the roads, blowing bridges and putting up roadblocks...

While this action was still in progress, after fierce fighting regular Soviet troops succeeded in breaking into our front line southwest of Nevel. As a result of the changed situation the Estonian SS Volunteer Brigade was given a new mission: intercept the Soviet units that had broken through. The brigade also helped seal off the point of penetration, its first action in the German main line of resistance. Its mission was to gain and hold a blocking position in the area of a narrows between two lakes...

Farther south, other units of the brigade launched an attack and smashed several breaches in an enemy defense position consisting of four lines. In the course of this fierce fighting a battery of 76.2-mm guns and five anti-tank guns plus numerous machine-guns and a large number of rifles were captured...

The Soviets suffered extremely heavy losses in this attack, which saw fierce hand-to-hand fighting."

Leo Sipelgas recalled of the action before Nevel:

"*New Year's Eve 1943 we—about 50 men—were sitting in a bunker of Headquarters, 46th SS Volunteer Grenadier Regiment and were just making preparations for the party. The table had just been set when two officers arrived. They had been sent by our regimental commander Tuuling to look for 10 volunteers for a special mission. I volunteered and soon afterward we were passing our positions at the edge of Lake Nesherda. On skis we easily crossed the ice toward a Russian-held island. We were supposed to take prisoners and if possible destroy several enemy positions. Everything went very quickly and an hour later we were back with two prisoners and two Maxim machine-guns. As well, we had destroyed two Soviet 76.2-mm guns with hand grenades. No sooner were we back in our positions, when Soviet guns began bombarding the island. We had been lucky and were even able to offer a toast to New Year 1944. Not long afterwards I was awarded the Iron Cross, Second Class at the Red Mill for having participated in this patrol action.*

One night at the beginning of February 1944 several Russians deserted to us with their field kitchen. They all still had weapons and there was corn mush in the field kitchen. They had appeared in front of the regimental headquarters without being noticed by any of us, which caused a minor sensation."

En route from Debica to the front in the Rosony area, October 1943.

Nevel

Bunker near Nevel.

Leo Sipelgas.

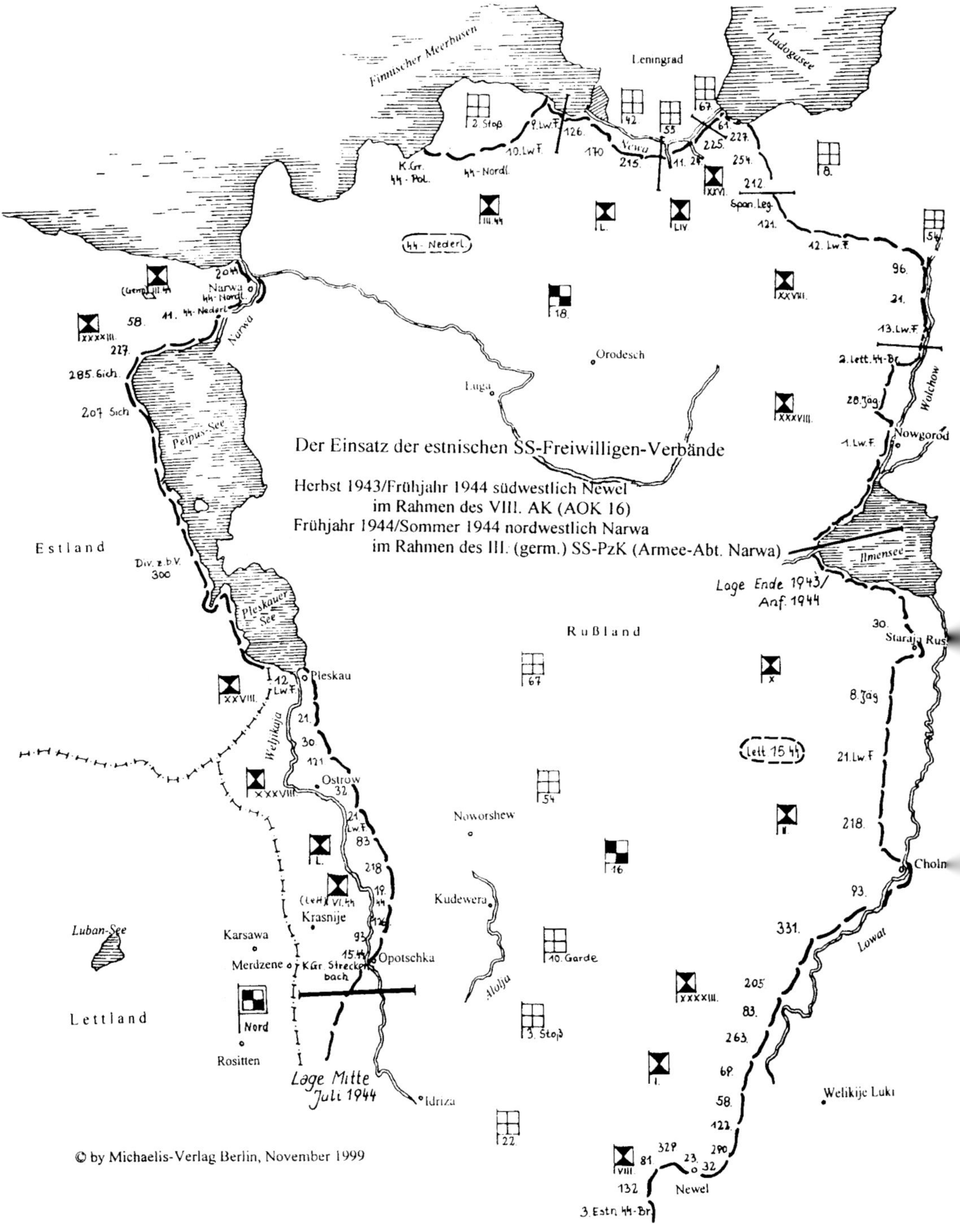

Actions involving the Estonian SS Volunteer Units

Autumn 1943-spring 1944 southwest of Nevel as part of VIII Army Corps (H.Q. 16th Army)

Spring 1944-summer 1944 northwest of Narva as part of III (Germanic) SS Panzer Corps (Army Detachment Narva)

Formation of the 20th Estonian SS Volunteer Division

On 24 January 1944 the SS-FHA ordered the 3rd Estonian SS Volunteer Brigade reorganized as the 20th Estonian SS Volunteer Division.[47] Chosen to command the unit was *SS-Standartenführer* Augsberger. The division initially retained its brigade organization with the 45th and 46th SS Volunteer Grenadier Regiments and existing brigade units. The 47th SS Volunteer Grenadier Regiment was to be formed later. Formation of the 20th SS Field Replacement Battalion, however, began immediately in Drissa at the front. The 14th Company of the 45th SS Volunteer Grenadier Regiment provided cadres for the anti-tank companies of the 45th, 46th, and 47th SS Volunteer Grenadier Regiments, the 1st Platoons were each to be equipped with three 75-mm Pak 40, the 2nd Platoons three 75-mm Pak 98/38, and the 3rd and 4th Platoons "Stovepipes" (bazookas). The 46th SS Volunteer Grenadier Regiment's 14th Company became 1st Company, 20th SS Anti-Tank Battalion. The 15th Companies of the two existing grenadier regiments were used to form the 20th SS Pioneer Battalion. While the signals units were supposed to be completely manned by Estonian personnel, German signals recruits were assigned to the 20th SS Signals Battalion, which was the reorganized 53rd SS Signals Company. The responsible replacement unit for Estonian personnel was the 33rd SS Grenadier Training and Replacement Battalion[33] (SS Training Camp Heidelager), and for the German members the 35th SS Grenadier Training and Replacement Battalion (SS Training Camp West Prussia). The division was to be organized as follows:

- Division Headquarters
- 45th SS Volunteer Grenadier Regiment (Estonian No. 1)
- 46th SS Volunteer Grenadier Regiment (Estonian No. 2)
- 47th SS Volunteer Grenadier Regiment (Estonian No. 3)
- 20th SS Volunteer Artillery Regiment (Estonian No. 1)
- 20th SS Fusilier Battalion
- 20th SS Anti-Tank Battalion
- 20th SS Flak Battalion
- 20th SS Signals Battalion
- 20th SS Pioneer Battalion

Dr. Mäe, then head of the Estonian self-administration, recalled of the general mobilization,[49] in which about 40,000 from the year classes 1904-1923 were drafted:[50]

"In autumn 1943 General-Commissar Litzmann telephoned and informed me that Himmler had arrived and wanted to speak to me. In the presence of the general-commissar

Himmler told me very amicably that a very broad autonomy had been worked out for Estonia and had been submitted to Hitler for signature. It was only a question of days before this was made public. However Hitler expected the Estonians to return the favor as a sign of good will.

What sign, I asked? Himmler's answered: we are in the fifth year of the war, numbers are all that matter now. You have many volunteers at the front, yet the Legion is numerically very weak. This is no way to build up a larger unit that will secure your future at the end of the war. You must take the step of introducing compulsory military service—that is, after all, part of your sovereignty you can be proud of. He said there was nothing standing in the way on the German side. I said that I would be happy if the coming autonomy gave us this right, for it is the right of an independent state…[51]

I signed a decree making Colonel Soodla, Inspector-General of the Estonian Legion, responsible for carrying out the mobilization. This authorized him to issue the necessary decrees with the approval of the General-Commissar. At about the same time Himmler made Soodla commander of the Waffen-SS replacement detachment in Estonia.

The German front before Leningrad collapsed in January 1944. German troops fled in panic. The Estonians were horrified, for it was winter, the sea was frozen and there was no way to flee. Senior SS and Police Commander Jeckeln telephoned me from Riga and invited me to attend a meeting there that same evening. Soodla received the same. On arriving in Riga we also met the General-Commissar of Estonia. The Latvians were represented at the meeting by General Bangerskis and another officer. Present were several senior German officers and officials. Senior SS and Police Commander Jeckeln presided and gave a speech. As he was visibly intoxicated, all we could gather from his slurred words was that there was nothing left defending the front and that no help was to be expected. Other officers gave a frank overview of the situation.

Jeckeln and Litzmann then turned to me and Bangerski and asked if we could help with domestic units, for the lives of our peoples were at stake. I asked for a break and discussed the matter with Soodla, while the Latvian officers did the same, after which we spoke with each other. It was obvious that our homelands were facing a catastrophic situation and we thought it best to take over the front ourselves where we could. If we had enough weapons and more forces than the Germans, it would be a favorable moment for us to take power ourselves, disarm the Germans and take independent political steps for our own protection. When the meeting resumed, therefore, General Bagerski and I said we would of course make every effort to defend our homelands. We then asked to be told how much materiel and weapons could be made available. Various representatives stated their available stocks and with that the meeting ended."

The transfer of the 20th Estonian SS Volunteer Division from the Sebesh sector of the front near Nevel began on 8 February 1944. The troop trains departed Opotschka for Dorpat, from where the division proceeded to Narva. There it was attached to Headquarters, III (Germanic) SS Panzer Corps (*SS-Obergruppenführer und General der Waffen-SS* Steiner[52]). On 28 February division commander Augsberger rated his unit as conditionally fit for offensive operations, but fully capable defensively. On the Narva front the division received numerous Estonian replacements. One, a former member of the Self-Defense Force, recalled:

"I was born in 1923 and, after finishing school, in July 1941 I joined the self-defense force—my father was a battalion commander in Fellin. At first we hunted Red Army stragglers in the forests and later I was made a guard at a prisoner of war camp in Fellin. Then in February 1944 I was transferred to the 20th Estonian SS Volunteer Division. I received six weeks of signals training in Hungerburg, after which I was assigned to the artillery regiment's headquarters battery."

On 14 March 1944, after completing the 11th wartime officer course at the SS Officer School in Bad Tölz, 35 Estonians were transferred to the 20th Estonian SS Volunteer Division. The next day 31 Estonian participants in the 3rd course for "Germanic officers" at Bad Tölz were ordered back to the division, whose strength on 17 April 1944, including the SS Volunteer Replacement Battalion and the already-attached Eastern Battalion 660, was:

Officers	NCOs	Enlisted Men	Total	
245	952	6,563	7,760	actual
3.2%	12.3%	84.5%	100%	
495	2,743	12,895	16,133	authorized
3%	17%	80%	100%	

Three months after the formation order the division had not even reached half its authorized strength. It was short 250 officers, 1,791 non-commissioned officers, and 6,332 enlisted men. At the end of the month in Kehra, the Estonian Eastern Battalions 658 and 659 were combined to form the 47th SS Volunteer Grenadier Regiment under the command of *Freiwilligen-Standartenführer* Vent. At the same time Eastern Battalion 660 became the 46th SS Volunteer Grenadier Regiment's III Battalion. The 45th SS Volunteer Grenadier Regiment's III Battalion was also formed at Camp Kehra from newly-drafted Estonians. Thus, in May 1944 the unit's strength was increased to about 10,000 members.

I Battalion, 45th SS Volunteer Grenadier Regiment at Meerapalu

During the transport of the 20th Estonian SS Volunteer Division to the Narva front by rail, I Battalion of the 45th SS Volunteer Grenadier Regiment under battalion commander *Freiwilligen-Sturmbannführer* Riipalu, reinforced by a platoon of pioneers and elements of the 20th SS Flak Battalion, was unloaded in Dorpat (Tartu) and attached to the 207th Security Division (*Generalleutnant* Erich von Hofmann[53]).[54] As the German command suspected that units of the Soviet 42nd Army (Colonel-General Masslenikov) were planning to cross the ice in the area of the Lake Peipus Peninsula, units were moved to the Meehikoorma River line. There the Estonian battalion was to be attached to Battle Group Gallas,[55] which had been formed from scratch units, and like them occupied quarters in abandoned villages.

In fact, the Red Army crossed frozen Lake Peipus to the west bank, bypassing the island of Piirissaar, and threatened the weak Battle Group Gallas. Because of snow-covered roads and inadequate transport, at first only the 4th Company was able to intervene in the fighting on 10-12 February 1944. *Oberst* Gallas subsequently intended to withdraw, but this idea was rejected by *Freiwilligen-Sturmbannführer* Riipalu, who wanted to drive the enemy back across the Estonian border. After a conversation with *Generalleutnant* von Hofmann, Riipalu assumed command of all German and Estonian units in the area.

After the roads had been cleared, allowing the three absent companies to join the 4th Company, the Estonians marched into the Meerapalu area. After a battalion of the 11th Infantry Division was added, the German-Estonian counterattack began there on 15 February 1944. To minimize casualties, Riipalu requested two Stuka attacks on the Soviet lines for 1255 and 1325 hours. The infantry attacked at 1335 and the village was taken at 1700. At the same time units of the 11th Infantry Division retook the island of Piirissaar. Two days later the 11th Infantry Division also took over the positions of SS Battle Group Riipalu, which left for Dorpat by truck. On 19 February 1944 the members of I Battalion, 45th SS Volunteer Grenadier Regiment joined the 20th Estonian SS Volunteer Division on the Narva, and on 24 February took over II Battalion's positions on the front line. The 207th Security Division moved its headquarters to Koosa, now responsible for guarding the west shore of Lake Peipus from the mouth of the Embach to Mustvee, a front of 60 km, plus the Baltic Coast on the Gulf of Finland from Toila to the Latvian border east of Riga.

Battles on the Narva[56]

(19 February – 19 September 1944)

On 19 February 1944 the Estonian units relieved the remnants of the 9th and 10th Field Divisions (L)[57] on the Narva. The positions held by II Battalion, 45th SS Volunteer Grenadier Regiment under *Freiwilligen-Hauptsturmführer* Maitla ran from Pähklamäe to Vepsküla. I Battalion, 46th SS Volunteer Grenadier Regiment under *Freiwilligen-Hauptsturmführer* Silvert was in Vepsküla, while the II Battalion under *SS-Obersturmführer* Weber was in the Riigi area. On 20 February I Battalion, 45th SS Volunteer Grenadier Regiment reached the division and was initially ordered into the Peeterristi area.

From 28 February to 3 March 1944 elements of the 45th SS Volunteer Grenadier Regiment—attached to the 11th SS Volunteer Panzer-Grenadier Division *Nordland*—attacked the Soviet bridgehead across the Narva near Vepsküla, and in close combat forced the Soviets back across the river and thus out of Estonia. On 9 March 1944 the *Wehrmacht* communiqué declared:

"*Southwest of Narva our counterattacks gained further ground in the face of stiff resistance. In several days of attacks, the 3rd Estonian SS Brigade under the command of SS-Oberführer Augsberger, together with Germanic volunteers of an SS panzer corps, eliminated the enemy's two Narva bridgeheads and inflicted heavy losses. Renewed attacks by the Soviets were repulsed with the loss of 14 tanks.*"

And two days later:

"*In the north of the Eastern Front the Bolsheviks attacked northwest of Nevel, in the Ostrov area, near Pskov and at Narva with powerful forces supported by tanks and aircraft. Their attempts to break through were thwarted by stubborn resistance from troops of the army and Estonian plus Latvian and Estonian SS volunteer units. Immediate counterattacks eliminated or sealed off local penetrations. The enemy lost 101 tanks.*"

On 16-17 March there was further fighting in which the Red Army succeeded in breaking into the positions of II Battalion, 45th SS Volunteer Grenadier Regiment. Counterattacks by I Battalion and elements of the 46th SS Volunteer Grenadier Regiment under *Freiwilligen-Standartenführer* Tuuling drove the Soviets back again. Fighting went on until the next day. This brought an end to the Soviet winter offensive in the 20th Estonian SS Volunteer Division's area, and with the end of the winter offensive Army Group North's entire front grew quiet. The corps and divisions were able to regroup and take in replacements. On 9 April 1944 the Estonian *Freiwilligen-Unterscharführer* Nugiseks[58] of I Battalion, 46th SS Volunteer Grenadier Regiment was awarded the Knight's Cross of the Iron Cross:

"I was born in Särevere-Karjaküla on 22 October 1921, and in October 1941 I joined the 185th Estonian Security Battalion. On 25 May 1943 I became a member of the Estonian SS Legion, and from 31 July to 16 October of that year I attended a course at the SS non-commissioned officer school in Lauenburg. I received the Iron Cross, Second Class on 27 February 1944 and ten days later the Iron Cross, First Class. Even I was surprised when I was awarded the Knight's Cross. I was in a hospital at the time, when suddenly my division commander Augsberger appeared with a number of photo reporters and hung the decoration around my neck. My promotion to Waffen-Oberscharführer was short-lived, however, as I had a run-in with some German military police who were treating several of my countrymen roughly. By August I was a Waffen-Unterscharführer again."

In June 1944 the later *Waffen-Unterscharführer* Lembit Jakuste was transferred from the *Wehrmacht* to the unit, by then renamed the 20th SS Waffen-Grenadier Division (Estonian No. 1):

"I was born in 1922 and studied forestry at Tartu University. In 1943 I voluntarily joined the Eastern Battalions' replacement battalion. The battalion commander was Oberstleutnant Fischer. I was posted to an anti-tank platoon (37-mm) assigned to guard the roads to Leningrad. In February 1944 we arrived at the Narva front. I spent the first three months training recruits called up in the general mobilization. In June 1944 I was ordered to the 20th SS Waffen-Grenadier Division at the front. After the heavy fighting in Estonia I went to the 20th SS Waffen-Artillery Regiment at the Neuhammer training camp and there became the 11th Battery's clerk. Finally, in May 1945 I was captured by the Soviets in Czechoslovakia."

Harald Nugiseks, concerning the latest renaming of the unit:

"The frequent name changes, first Estonian SS Legion, then Estonian SS Volunteer Brigade, Estonian SS Volunteer Division and finally SS Waffen-Grenadier Division didn't bother us. Few cared whether we were designated Legions-Unterscharführer (etc.) or Freiwilligen-Unterscharführer or Waffen-Unterscharführer or even SS-Untersturmführer. What we desired most was to serve in a national army of our own and not under the banner of the Waffen-SS."

The 47th SS Waffen-Grenadier Regiment arrived at the Narva front from Kehra shortly before the start of the Soviet summer offensive on 22 June 1944. Its II Battalion took over the positions of the 45th SS Waffen-Grenadier Regiment, which together with the 20th SS Fusilier Battalion relieved troops of the 126th Infantry Division south of Auvere.[60] I Battalion, 47th SS Waffen-Grenadier Regiment also moved into the area south of Auvere and was attached to the 11th SS Volunteer Panzer-Grenadier Division *Nordland*. The 46th SS Waffen-Grenadier Regiment had extended its positions to the sea alongside II Battalion, 47th SS Waffen-Grenadier Regiment.

As Himmler intended to bring all Estonians serving in the *Wehrmacht* and police into the *Waffen-SS*, he decreed that formation of the second Estonian SS waffen-grenadier division should begin west of Lake Peipus on 15 July 1944. Each of the three existing grenadier regiments was to provide a battalion to

The Fighting in Estonia

Summer 1944

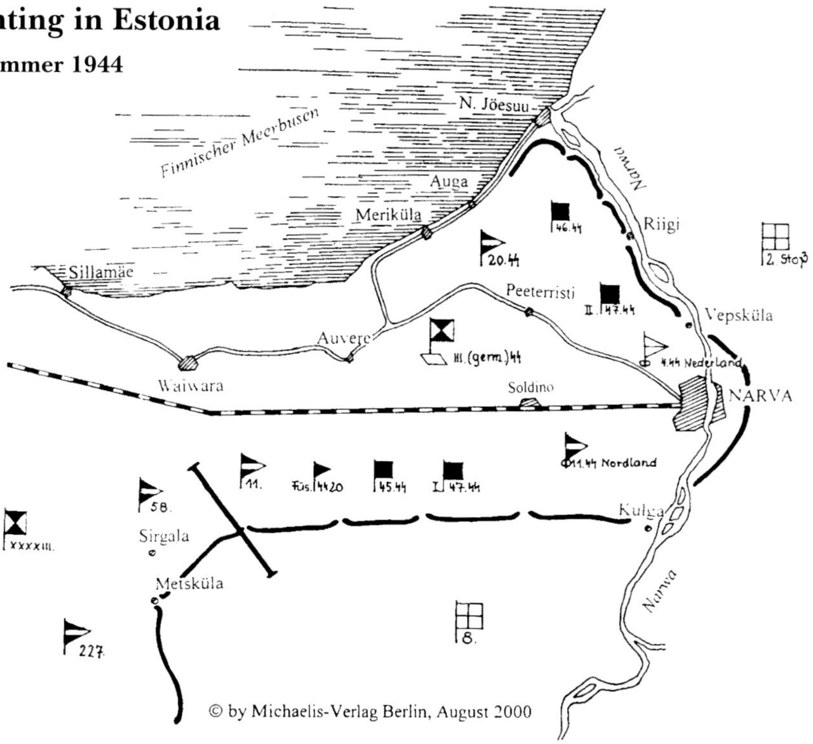

serve as formation cadre, while the resulting shortfall in men was to be made good by the SS border police regiments. The designated commander of the division (sic!), which was supposed to become operational in two months, was *SS-Oberführer* Lombard. At the same time, the SS-FHA was making plans to form a Headquarters, X SS Waffen Army Corps (Estonian). The big Soviet offensive and the resulting developments in the situation meant that neither the division nor corps was created.

At 0500 hours on 25 July 1944, following an hour-long artillery barrage, units of Marshall Govorov's Leningrad Front (2nd Shock Army and 8th Army) launched an attack against *Armee-Abteilung Narwa*. At 1000 hours enemy troops broke into the positions held by the Estonian units south of Auvere, however, the 20th SS Fusilier Battalion launched a counterattack and temporarily retook the positions.

On the Narva the enemy attacked at Vasa, Riigi, and Hungerburg. On that day the war diary of the 4th SS Volunteer Panzer-Grenadier Brigade *Nederland* noted:

"*Report by the operations officer/20. Waffen-Grenadier-Division der SS. Russians have 1 battalion across the Narva at Vasa and on both sides of Riigi. Bridging in progress at Vasa. He is requesting assistance...*"

With assistance from the 4th SS Volunteer Panzer-Grenadier Brigade this attack was sealed off on a line from Auga (coast) to Purjya (main road). In the course of shortening the front, on 26 July the III (Germanic) SS Panzer Corps abandoned its positions on the Narva and pulled back into a new defense line, the so-called "Tannenberg Position," eight kilometers farther west. The Estonian troops withdrew through Soldino and Auvere via the Narva—Wesenburg—Olgino—Peeterristi—Luagna—Repniku road and the Narva to Wesenberg rail line.

The front now ran from the Gulf of Finland south across the Narva to Reval highway. Anchoring the defense line were three pieces of high ground in the Blue Mountains: Orphanage Hill in the east, Grenadier Hill in the west, and Hill 69.9. The 20th SS Waffen-Grenadier Division, which had been battered in the fighting, was assembled in the Sillamäe—Waiwara area, supposedly to gain some rest as corps reserve. In fact, however, the Mummaassaare sector right on the coast was almost immediately handed over to the II Battalion of the 47th Waffen-Grenadier Regiment. As a result, from north to south the main line of resistance was manned by:

II Battalion/47th SS Waffen-Grenadier Regiment
54th SS Pioneer Battalion
49th SS Volunteer Panzer-Grenadier Regiment
II and III Battalions/24th SS Volunteer Panzer-Grenadier Regiment
III Battalion/23rd SS Volunteer Panzer-Grenadier Regiment
elements of the 11th Infantry Division

On Orphanage Hill, Grenadier Hill, and Hill 69.9 were:

SS Assault Brigade Langenmarck
two companies of the 11th SS Volunteer Panzer-Grenadier Division

On 27 July 1944 troops of the Soviet 2nd Shock Army and the 8th Army attacked Orphanage Hill. Local penetrations were counterattacked and eliminated. To avoid the threat of encirclement the German troops pulled back towards Grenadier Hill, suffering heavy casualties. The next day a counterattack by I Battalion, 47th SS Waffen-Grenadier Regiment to regain the lost hill collapsed under enemy fire and the battalion commander, *Waffen-Sturmbannführer* Sooden, was killed. When the Red Army again tried to break through to the west along the highway, the 45th SS Waffen-Grenadier Regiment was also sent into action in the Blue Mountains. The enemy gained little ground. On 29 July 1944 100 enemy tanks of various types overran the defense positions and took Grenadier Hill; however, by the evening elements of the 45th SS Waffen-Grenadier Regiment succeeded in retaking the vital hill in fierce fighting. The ferocity of the fighting and the resulting high casualties were reflected in the fighting strengths. For example, after the fighting in the Blue Mountains II Battalion, 45th SS Waffen-Grenadier Regiment had an effective strength of just 48 men!

In the first three days of August there were further heavy Soviet attacks on the entire front. The defenders, by summoning the last of their strength, managed to hold. On 1 August 1944 the OKW reported:

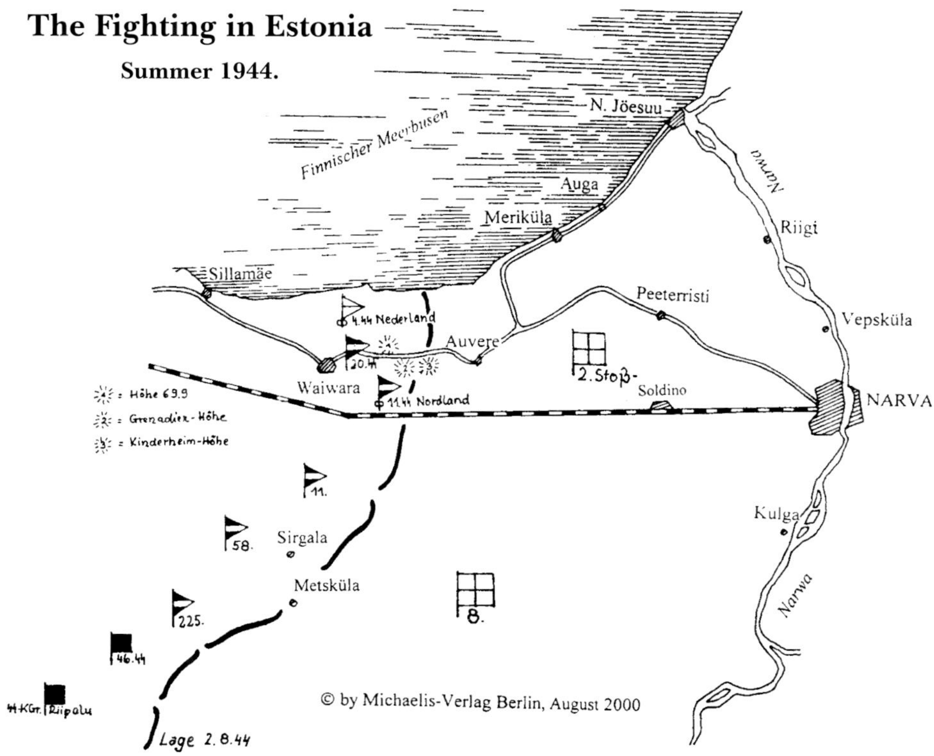

"In the Narva Isthmus the enemy did not continue his major offensive yesterday because of heavy losses. Weaker attacks failed. The III (Germanic) SS Panzer Corps under the command of SS-Obergruppenführer und General der Waffen-SS Steiner with the Germanic Volunteer Divisions SS Nordland and SS Nederland, the 20th Estonian SS Volunteer Division, the 11th East Prussian Infantry Division, units of the navy deployed on the land front, and army artillery and rocket batteries, has played an outstanding role in the successful defense against the Soviet offensive in recent days."

The war diary of the 4th SS Volunteer Panzer-Grenadier Brigade *Nederland* also praised the fighting strength of the Estonians:

"The Ostland Naval Operational Battalion under the command of Kapitänleutnant Ditscher and II Battalion of the 47th SS Waffen-Grenadier Regiment under the command of Waffen-Sturmbannführer Rebane distinguished themselves through conspicuous bravery and steadfastness in the defensive fighting of the past days in which extremely heavy losses were inflicted on the enemy."

It is acknowledged that a unit is only as good as its officers, and on 2 August 1944 SS war correspondent *SS-Untersturmführer* Kurbjuhn reported on shortcomings of command in the 46th SS Waffen-Grenadier Regiment and the poor morale among many Estonian members of the 20th SS Waffen-Grenadier Division:

"SS-Rgt. 46 suffered heavy casualties because of errors in command[61]*. Almost completely encircled, it fled in panic, leaving the flank open, resulting in the near destruction of SS-Rgt. 48. SS-Rgt. 47 stepped in and restored the situation at the cost of heavy casualties. Morale in the division is very low. The word going round is: `Germany is abandoning Estonia!'*

1,571 Estonians deserted in July 1944, including 23 officers. III SS Panzer Corps is of the opinion that the division is no longer completely reliable."

The III (Germanic) SS Panzer Corps thus viewed the division as no longer reliable, while at the same time the highest praise was being expressed for individual units and battle groups!

When Soviet forces broke through the positions of the 170th and 225th Infantry Divisions near Metsküla—Putki, the 46th SS Waffen-Grenadier Regiment, now under the command of *Waffen-Obersturmbannführer* Rebane, plus SS Battle Group Riipalu made up of the I Battalion/45th SS Waffen-Grenadier Regiment, the 20th SS Fusilier Battalion, and the 111th Security Regiment, plus elements of the 227th Infantry Division, were ordered to seal off the threatened sector of the front, and in fierce fighting the Estonians carried out the order. The positions were handed back to the *Wehrmacht* and the units sent farther south for further action.

SS Battle Groups Rebane and Vent

On 18 July 1944 the front between Ostrov and the southern tip of Lake Pskov was shattered. On 10 August the 3rd Baltic Front (Army General Masslenikov) launched a further attack against the left wing of the XXVII Army Corps on the 18th Army's left flank. The Soviets drove the 21st, 30th, and 121st Infantry Divisions and the 21st *Luftwaffe* Field Division back beyond Petseri, and in the evening reached the area east of Voru, where there were no more German troops.

On 14 August 1944, *Armee-Abteilung Narwa* (Army Detachment Narva), tasked by Army Group North with barring the way between Lake Peipus and Lake Wirz, ordered the recently-attached 207th Security Division[62] to hold the narrows between the lakes near Mehikoorma and to the south for as long as possible and establish a south-facing blocking position in the area of the Vöhandu River. A planned attack by the German XXVIII Army Corps (18th Army) to close the gap to Army Detachment Narva was cancelled, as the troops in the north had already pulled back towards the Vöhandu position. In order to restore contact between the 207th Security Division and the troops of the XXVIII Army Corps, on 14 August 1944 orders were issued for the formation of SS Battle Group Vent. It consisted of I Battalion, 45th SS Waffen-Grenadier Regiment and I and II Battalions, 46th SS Waffen-Grenadier Regiment, and was attached to the division-strength SS Battle Group Wagner. Under the command of *SS-Brigadeführer und Generalmajor der Waffen-SS* Wagner, commanding officer of the 4th SS Volunteer Panzer-Grenadier Brigade *Nederland*, the battle group consisted of:

the 54th SS Signals Company
the 54th SS Military Police Squad
the 54th SS Workshop Platoon
I Battalion, 45th SS Waffen-Grenadier Regiment
I Battalion, 46th SS Waffen-Grenadier Regiment
II Battalion, 46th SS Waffen-Grenadier Regiment
the battle group of the 5th Company, SS Volunteer Assault Brigade *Wallonien*
the 23rd Grenadier Regiment
one battery of the 1004th Army Coastal Artillery Battalion
III Battalion, 3rd Rocket Regiment
II Battalion, 58th Artillery Regiment
the 11th SS Armored Reconnaissance Battalion
one company of the 54th SS Anti-Tank Battalion

The battle group marched into the area between the right wing of the 207th Security Division, which had been placed under its command, and the left wing of the XXVIII Army Corps near Pölva.

Also formed, to meet an anticipated landing by the 2nd Baltic Front in the Meerapalu and Mehikoorma sector with the objective of advancing on Dorpat and cutting off the German forces to the south, was SS Battle Group Rebane. It consisted of:

II Battalion, 47th SS Waffen-Grenadier Regiment
the 11th Fusilier Battalion
a light artillery battalion of the 11th Infantry Division
II and III Battalions, 5th SS Border Police Regiment

It was transported by rail into the Tartu area. From there the battle group was sent to Luunja, where it occupied a second line between Melliste and Vonnu.

The Soviets made a successful landing near Mehikoorma, on the western shore of Lake Peipus, at dawn on 16 August 1944. They met little resistance from the two Estonian SS border police regiments, which were under the command of *Oberst* Gallas. In the afternoon SS Battle Group Wagner launched a counterattack with the objective of reducing the enemy bridgehead on the western shore of Lake Peipus. The attack was unsuccessful, and the situation forced the German-Estonian units to pull back to the Ahja position. A member of the 207th Security Division recalled the fighting:

"On the afternoon of 18 August 1944 the enemy division which had crossed the Mehikoorma narrows on 16 August attacked the Ahja River line near Lääniste and drove the Estonians back towards Vonnu. The division's panzer company saved the situation with a vigorous counterattack, which caught the Russian infantry in the middle of their attack and completely decimated them. As a result, we were able to lead the Estonians[63] into prepared trenches east of Vonnu and motivate them to hold..."

On 21 August 1944 the 1st, 54th, and 67th Shock Armies of the 3rd Baltic Front attacked north between Dorpat and Walk with the objective of linking up with the Leningrad Front near Reval. Fierce fighting developed on the eastern shore of Lake Wirz and contact between the 18th Army and Army Detachment Narva was severed for good. The next day III Battalion, 46th SS Waffen-Grenadier Regiment,[64] made up of Estonians who had formerly served in the Finnish 200th Infantry Regiment, arrived in Dorpat and was attached to the 87th Infantry Division.[65] The German-Estonian troops received orders to withdraw beyond the Emajogi River and occupy a new defense position there.

On 24 August 1944, however, enemy troops succeeded in advancing across the intact bridge over the Emajogi at Karavere. After fierce street fighting with elements of the 11th Infantry Division, the battle group of the 5th SS Volunteer Grenadier Brigade *Wallonien* and Estonian units, they were able to occupy Dorpat and establish a bridgehead across the river. The positions along the Emajogi remained quiet until 17 September 1944 when, after a heavy artillery bombardment, the enemy launched his offensive in the direction of Reval. SS Battle Group Rebane, along with other units, including elements of the 5th SS Border Police Regiment, was surrounded in the morning hours. By the evening of the next day, however, the men were able to pull back to their own main line of resistance. In the process

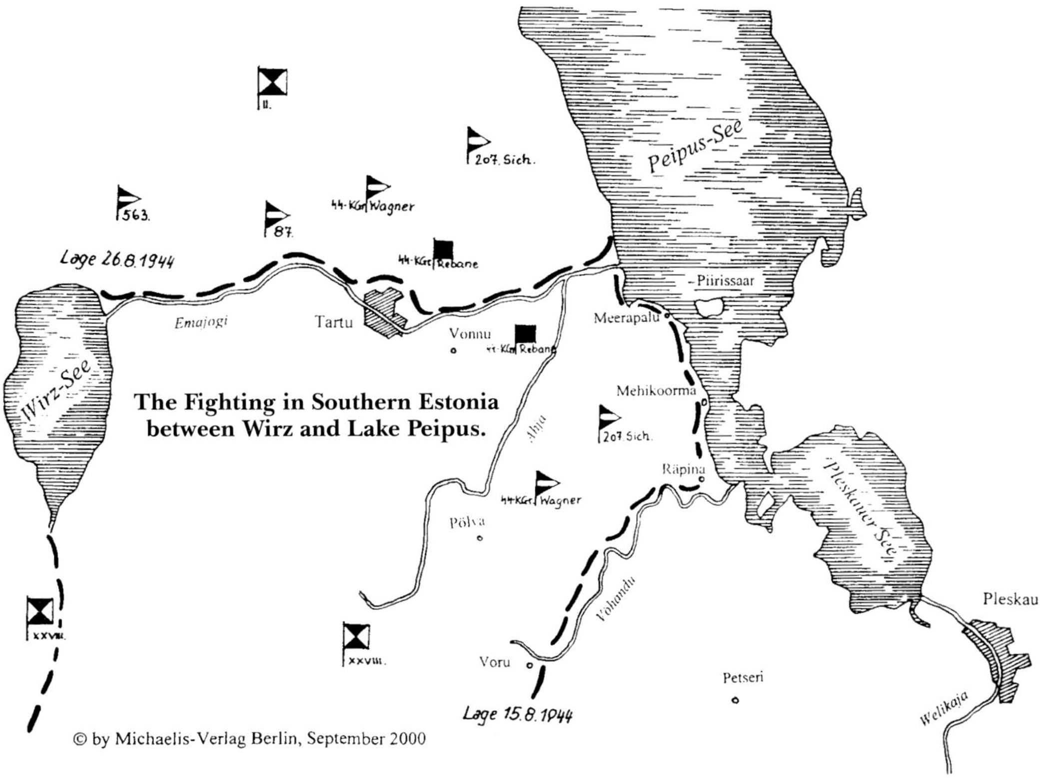

The Fighting in Southern Estonia between Wirz and Lake Peipus.

there was a confrontation with the VIII Estonian Rifle Corps (Lieutenant-General Pern), which had been established by the Red Army. Estonians in Soviet units were fighting against Estonians in German units!

The units of the 20th SS Waffen Grenadier Division (Estonian No. 1),[66] in the Estonian southern front, namely the:

I Battalion, 45th SS Waffen-Grenadier Regiment
I and II Battalions, 47th SS Waffen-Grenadier Regiment
II Battalion, 46th SS Waffen-Grenadier Regiment

received orders to march via Jögeva into the Rakke—Koeru area and join the remaining division elements there.

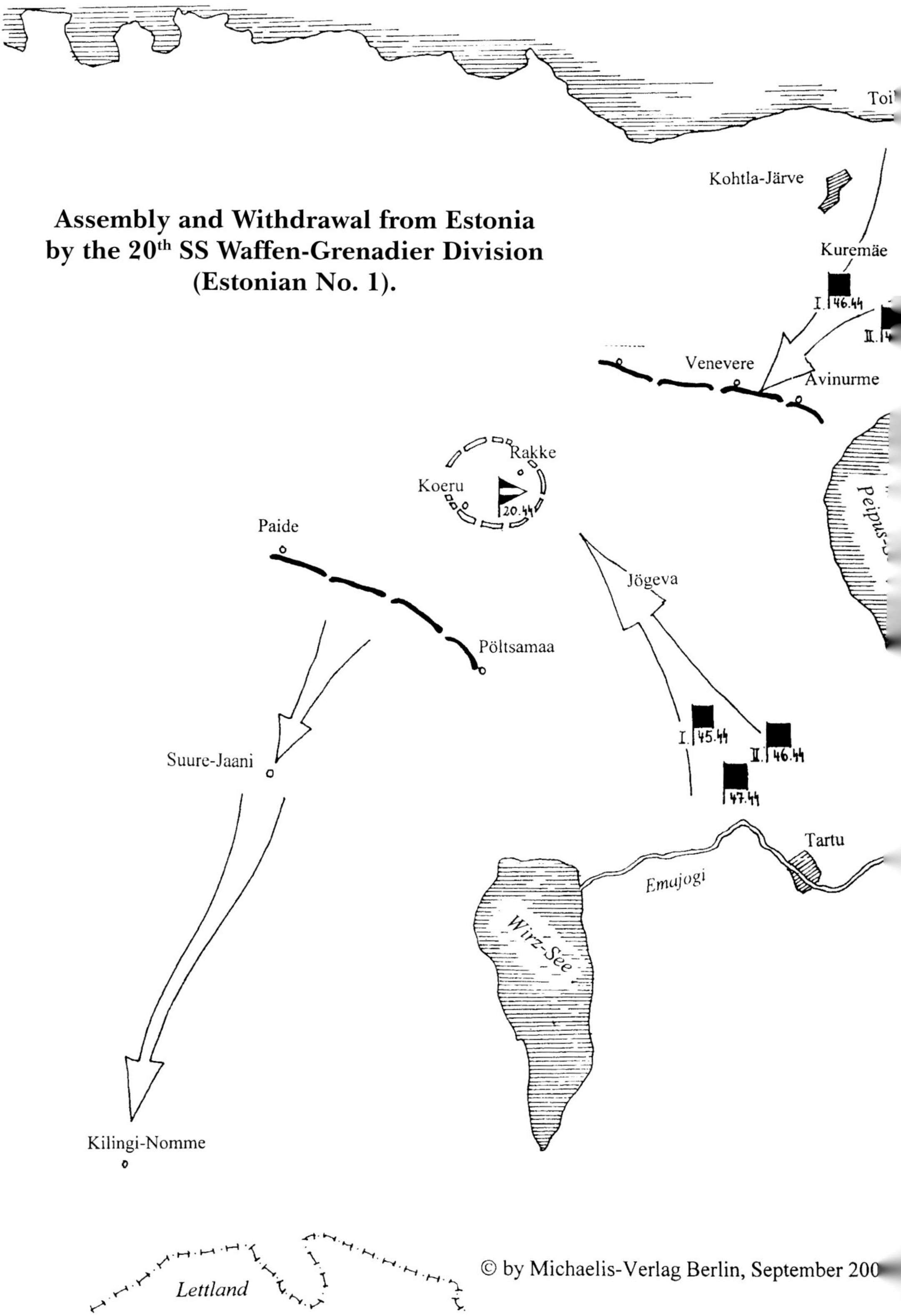
Assembly and Withdrawal from Estonia
by the 20th SS Waffen-Grenadier Division
(Estonian No. 1).
Toi
Kohtla-Järve
Kuremäe
I. 46.44
Venevere
Avinurme
Rakke
Koeru
20.44
Paide
Jögeva
Pöltsamaa
Peipus-
I. 45.44
II. 46.44
47.44
Suure-Jaani
Tartu
Emajogi
Wirz-See
Kilingi-Nomme
Lettland
© by Michaelis-Verlag Berlin, September 200

The Retreat from Estonia

By the beginning of September 1944 the Red Army's attacks had eased off, as it regrouped for further operations. The offensive in southern Estonia began on 17 September 1944, while on the Narva front things remained quiet. To prevent a foreseeable encirclement of Army Detachment Narva, however, on 18 September 1944 Army Group North ordered "Operation Aster," the evacuation of the Narva Front and Estonia.

At nightfall on that day the III (Germanic) SS Panzer Corps—the heavy weapons first—was to withdraw toward Pernau. The final elements were to leave the area east of Wesenberg the next day. Having left the Tannenberg Position, II Battalion, 45th SS Waffen-Grenadier Regiment reached Kuremäe at noon on 18 September. In the afternoon I Battalion, 46th SS Waffen-Grenadier Regiment, which had assembled in a forest near Toila, encountered I Battalion, 45th SS Waffen-Grenadier Regiment. The division command post, which primarily commanded these two regiments plus those elements of the division—mainly supply units—not deployed in the southern front, was located near Koeru.

On 20 September 1944 the SS-FHA reported the strength of the division without the four battalions attached to SS Battle Group Wagner as:

Officers	NCOs	Enlisted Men	Total	
439	1,978	12,965	15,382	actual
2.8%	12.9%	84.3%	100%	
474	2,590	11,634	14,698	authorized
3.2%	17.6%	79.2%	100%	

If one adds the four absent battalions to the calculations, with the numerous additions from the Eastern and Police Battalions the division's strength was about 18,000 members. It is noteworthy that there were 566 Russian *Hiwis* (auxiliaries) in the division at that time. This figure later increased to 892!

On that day Augsberger flew to Berlin to see Himmler and discuss the future of his division.[67] He knew what it meant for the Estonian members that on the one side the German *Wehrmacht* was evacuating Estonia, and on the other that they were now to abandon their homeland and leave their families defenseless against the invading Soviets. When he returned to Estonia on 21 September he brought with him Himmler's agreement that while as many Estonian members of the division as possible were to be evacuated to Germany, it was not to be a priority.

At the same time the division, assembled in the Rakke – Koeru area, was ordered to move into the Avinurme – Venevere – Simuna area. There, together with Headquarters, 300th Special Purpose Division, it was to establish a north-facing front to enable Army Detachment Narva to withdraw in the direction of Pernau.

The very next day the Estonian SS Waffen-Grenadier regiments pulled back toward the line Paide – Pöltsamaa as per orders. A number of soldiers were captured by the Soviets, including *SS-Obersturmführer* Hando Ruus,[68] commander of the 20th SS Fusilier Battalion.

To maintain better control over the units and thus be able to combat signs of disintegration, the Estonians were taken out of action and sent to Latvia. The war diary of the 4th SS Volunteer Panzer-Grenadier Brigade *Nederland* noted of the attachment of the 20th SS Flak Battalion and the general mood of the Estonian soldiers:

"As per telex from Headquarters, III Panzer Corps the following are immediately placed under the brigade's command: 20th SS Flak Battalion and Battle Commander Pernau. Commander 20th SS Flak Battalion reports that elements of the Estonian units only want to keep fighting if they are in Estonia. Signs of unrest are appearing among the Estonian Border Police units, which in some cases are shooting at German soldiers[69]*..."*

On 24 September 1944 the 20th SS *Waffen-Grenadier* Division marched south through Suure-Jaani, and the next day arrived at the Latvian border near Klinge-Nomme. It was incorporated into the 16th Army and ordered into the Riga area. Approximately 50% of the Estonian members of the division remained in their homeland, in no small part because of rumors that, following agreements with the western allies, the Red Army was only going to be in the country for several weeks and then withdraw.

The III (Germanic) SS Panzer Corps was combined with Corps Group Kleffel and the XXXIX Panzer Corps to form Army Detachment Grasser, whose job it was to maintain contact with the 3rd Panzer Army. Army Group North, ordered its forces to man the Segewold Position, which extended from the Bay of Riga north of Riga east toward Segewold, and there turned southwest through Baldone to Mitau. After the Segewold Position had been manned, it was possible to withdraw several divisions from the front line.[70]

On 26 September Headquarters, 16th Army asked the army group command for the removal of the 20th SS Waffen-Grenadier Division from Riga, as it represented a danger in its eyes. The division was fragmented, and the majority of its members resigned after the loss of their homeland. After the Soviet occupation of 1940-41 the men could imagine how their families would be treated. Former *Waffen-Untersturmführer* Walter Valtin (20th SS Waffen-Artillery Regiment) recalled the retreat from Estonia:

"After the reorganization of the 3rd Estonian SS Volunteer Brigade into the 20th Estonian SS Volunteer Division, beginning on 15 August 1944 I saw action on the Narva front. On 17 September 1944 my unit (horse-drawn howitzer battery) began pulling back from the swamps south of the Tannenberg Line. One gun stayed in position and laid down harassing fire all night. The guns were transported in two pieces—barrel and carriage separately. Each piece was pulled by six draft horses. We were forced to stick to forest roads and sandy side roads, as the main roads were being kept open for the motorized troops. The horses had to work hard. On the second day we were supposed to establish a firing position, and I readied my squad to set up an observation post about two kilometers away. But the whole thing was called off and our retreat resumed. Finally we came to a better road that led south. We were soon forced to leave it, however, for only the motorized units—meaning the

Narva, spring 1944.

***Waffen-Brigadeführer* Soodla (front right).**

Spring 1944.

81.4-mm mortar.

The SS Battle Group Riipalu during transfer to Dorpat.

Summer 1944.

Estonian volunteers in summer 1944.

Quick conference.

Summer 1944.

Estonian non-commissioned officers and enlisted men.

Field kitchen near Narva.

Transport to Narva.

SS-Obergruppenführer Steiner presents *Waffen-Obersturmbannführer* Riipalu with the Knight's Cross awarded him on 23/8/1944.

The Herrmannn Fortress.

On the Narva Front.

Landscape near Jõgeva.

The Blue Mountains.

Ivangorod Castle (Russia).

German units and baggage trains—were being sent through Viljandi. Early in the morning we passed a small town with a large slaughterhouse. There we picked up several sacks filled with various kinds of sausage. As it was absolutely necessary to give the horses a long rest and feed them properly, we spent the night in a home economics school. At dawn a dispatch rider arrived from the regiment and delivered orders for us to proceed as quickly as possible to a small city on the Estonian-Latvian border.

After a few hours I realized that the path of our retreat was going to take us near to my parents' house, and so I asked my battery commander for permission to visit my home. He gave me a day's leave after I gave my word of honor to return. A gun commander loaned me a riding horse and I trotted ahead of the battery to home. That was on 22 September 1944. Of course my family was astonished when I suddenly turned up. Afterwards I also visited several neighbors. Everyone was extremely upset, for they expected the Russians to arrive at any time. I left at dusk. After the preceding events both I and my horse were tired. I slept in the saddle. When I awoke my horse was standing in the middle of the road, its head hanging down. I spurred the animal on, but soon afterwards the same thing happened again. After a pause I rode on and rejoined my battery in Kilingi-Nomme just as it was getting light. Everyone there was extremely agitated. It was finally clear that we had to leave Estonia, our homes and our families. A few small groups took their small arms, plenty of ammunition and food, intending to take to the forests as guerillas to protect their families.

Toward noon four 8-ton prime movers arrived and picked up our guns. I was able to ride, as I had been made a gun commander…"

Reformation of the 20th SS Waffen-Grenadier Division (Estonian No. 1)

(15 October 1944 to 31 January 1945)

On 6 October 1944 the SS-FHA ordered the division transferred to the Neuhammer training camp for reformation.[71] When the Estonians learned of this, some deserted from their units to return home and there possibly fight as partisans against the Soviets. While the bulk of the division was transported to Germany by ship, the heavy units in particular drove southwest. On 7 October 1944 Headquarters Rothkirch reported to Headquarters, Army Group North that 138 officers, 395 non-commissioned officers, and 1,158 enlisted men of the 20th SS Waffen-Grenadier Division had so far arrived at the Estonian-Latvian border in the area of Skoudas, along with 40 officers, 50 NCOs, and 128 enlisted men from other Estonian units.[72] On 10 October these Estonian units crossed the Latvian border with the German Reich near Krottingen, and several days later arrived at the Neuhammer training camp. There the division was to become operational again by 30 May 1945—or after eight months. Walter Valtin recalled:

"After two-and-a-half days we came to a camp near Frauenburg, east of Libau. The prime movers left us and at first we were left alone with our guns. A week later we handed our guns over to a Wehrmacht unit remaining in Courland, while we were transferred to Memel. We passed through the abandoned city in the direction of East Prussia. Memel was the first German city `temporarily' evacuated. All of the doors of the houses were open, behind them meticulously clean emptied rooms. I remember clearly standing before a large shop window, gazing at the display of countless women's shoes, something we hadn't seen in over four years. Near noon the column stopped; the Russians had reached the Baltic near Heydekrug and cut off our way to East Prussia. By evening we were back in Memel and headed for the harbor. There they began shipping people to the Kurische Nehrung, first the refugees, then the military. All the while a Russian long-range gun fired randomly into the city. I waited with about 50 men in a shed approximately 60 meters from the loading quay. At about 23:00 a shell struck the quay and injured our regimental commander, Waffen-Obersturmbannführer Sobolev, the commander of I Battalion, Waffen-Sturmbannführer Vöhma, and several men. Sobolev died in hospital a week later. Vöhma later showed up at Neuhammer and led the regiment until SS-Obersturmbannführer Belzer arrived.

Our turn came in the morning and we were transported across the approximately three-kilometer-wide haff (lagoon). There followed a foot march down the approximately 96-kilometer-long Kurische Nehrung to Königsberg. We made this in 2.5 days, and we were quartered on the Labiau Estate for several days. Then we marched to Großraum Station and on 30 October 1944 arrived at the Neuhammer training camp. I fell ill at that time and remained in hospital until the end of the war—lastly in Schleswig-Holstein."

The training camp was also a catch basin for all Estonian units. This led to a dispute between *SS-Brigadeführer* Augsberger and Colonel Sinka, commander of the Estonian Self-Defense Force, who refused to allow his men to be attached to the division. Augsberger subsequently went straight to the SS Head Office in Berlin—after his return the Self-Defense Force was incorporated lock, stock, and barrel into the 20th SS Waffen-Grenadier Division. At first the enlisted men were remustered, with the younger ones assigned to the rifle companies of the 45th and 46th Waffen-Grenadier Regiments. Some men were sent on NCO courses; however, the officers of the border police had to take an officer's course given by the division to determine their suitability and future employment.

In addition to individual and group training, unit exercises resumed. After the bulk of the Estonians from the Border Police, Police and Self-Defense units had been transferred to the *Waffen-SS*, on 1 December 1944 they swore an oath to Hitler. A former member recalled:

"*The entire division, including the 20th SS Training and Replacement Regiment, assembler at Neuhammer. The division commander, SS-Brigadeführer Augsberger, gave a short speech. He declared that never before had so many Estonian soldiers been assembled as today at Neuhammer training camp. That was a fact…*

Before we sang the song of allegiance, SS-Untersturmführer Reitel climbed onto an assault gun and, with the help of a sword, assumed the role of conductor.

After the oath there was a parade before the division commander and guests. The officer's course led the marchpast and Waffen-Sturmbannführer Kappus carried the flag."

At that time the unit consisted of about 11,000 Estonians and 150 German officers, 750 non-commissioned officers, and 1,600 enlisted men. Total strength was thus about 13,500 men.

On 20 December 1944 the General of Volunteer Units in the OKH decreed that all Estonian auxiliaries serving in the *Wehrmacht* were to be transferred to the *Reichsführer-SS* and had to be sent to Neuhammer. From them the 47th SS Waffen-Grenadier Regiment was reformed, however, events prevented it from being armed and equipped. A former German member recalled:

"*The evacuated elements of the 20th SS Waffen-Grenadier Division assembled themselves at Neuhammer training camp in October-November 1944.*

During a meeting of officers Augsberger stressed that not a hair must be harmed on any of the Estonians' heads—no matter what their behavior during the retreat—and they were therefore also not subject to court-martial proceedings. Augsberger also declared that he would rather agree to a transfer of the German personnel than blame something on the Estonians.

The incoming flow of personnel caused a problem, namely housing. There would probably have been room for the men in the training camp, but the families! And so it was that some of the men camped in tents and caves in the woods, which once again resulted in the men leaving their posts to be with their families and becoming unavailable for duty. As per Augsberger's order they could not be punished, and the whole thing was one big headache for the junior officers.

Once conditions had somewhat normalized themselves again, work on rebuilding the division finally began. That was still before Christmas 1944. The 47th Regiment was in a barracks complex inside the training camp. The men were transferred to the regiment a few at a time and immediately used to form cadres for the companies that were to be established. Unfortunately no papers came with the men, so that one never knew with whom he was dealing with, especially as there were no translators available. To put it simply, it was a mess!

When the Russian launched his big offensive from the Baranov bridgehead, the division was alerted. Orders were received to transfer all usable men and weapons from the 47th Regiment to the 45th and 46th Regiments in exchange for all the sick. Once again all this happened without papers or identity discs..."

Former *SS-Unterscharführer* Wilhelm Barenscheer recalled:

"I was born in the Lüneburg Heath in 1922 and in 1940 I volunteered for the Waffen-SS. In April 1941 I was called up by the SS Anti-Tank Replacement Battalion and in June of that year was transferred to the Reichsführer-SS Escort Battalion in Oranienburg. From Rastenburg, in August 1941 we came to Arys training camp in East Prussia.

After actions before Leningrad and at the Volkhov—where I received the Iron Cross, Second Class—we were sent to France. There we were given 75-mm anti-tank guns and prime movers. One day I was summoned by name and transferred to Debica training camp to act as an instructor for the Estonian SS Panzer-Grenadier Battalion Narva.

I was actually supposed to then help in the establishment of the Hitlerjugend SS Panzer-Grenadier Division, but I remained with the Estonians and then saw action at Nevel with the 3rd Estonian SS Volunteer Brigade.

I subsequently saw further action in spring 1944 with 15th Company, 46th SS Volunteer Grenadier Regiment and also took part in the action in the Dorpat area, where we were cut off by the Russians for a time.

During the retreat from Estonia, almost all of the Estonians in our company disappeared overnight—so I was forced to drive a truck onto which had been loaded a Kübelwagen and three motorcycles. We drove from Mittau to Königsberg and from there were transported by rail to Neuhammer. I was awarded the war Merit Cross, 2nd Class for bringing back a total of five vehicles."

After the start of the Soviet 1945 winter offensive, the Estonians were alerted after just three months of training and sent as a battle group to Silesia. All that remained of the division at Neuhammer was division headquarters, the nascent 47th SS Waffen-Grenadier Regiment[73] and the 20th SS Waffen-Grenadier Training and Replacement Regiment (commanding officer *Waffen-Sturmbannführer* Koort).[74]

The Herrmann Fortress.

***SS-Brigadeführer* Augsberger and *Waffen-Obersturmbannführer* Riipalu inspect members of the division in Neuhammer, December 1944.**

SS Battle Group Rehfeldt

When Soviet troops broke through the Steinau bridgehead, on 6 February 1945 the remaining troops at Neuhammer were combined to form Battle Group Rehfeldt, consisting of three rifle companies. As there was neither a main line of resistance nor any coherent group of forces in the area, the Estonians and a Hungarian SS battle group were sent to the Bober River. A former German officer recalled:

"That same day we marched along the autobahn until we came to the Zumm forester's house, where we were going to leave the autobahn and head north. In this wooded terrain we were supposed to work our way forward to the positions at the Bober and relieve the police who were supposedly there. But we never made it to the positions, because we ran straight into the Russians in these forests. There was a terrific outburst of firing and our poorly trained and armed men immediately fled to the rear, and even we officers were caught up in the flight. After a few hundred meters we drew our guns and were finally able to stop the men, but many had already disappeared never to be seen again...

Our unit was commanded by an army Hauptmann serving with the 20th SS Waffen-Grenadier Division. We overheard the Hauptmann's conversation with SS-Obersturmbannführer Rehfeldt over the still-intact line to the training camp: SS-Obersturmbannführer , I am unable to hold the positions, the men are running away in droves.[75] *Reply: I couldn't care less, you are responsible for your men, that's why you're an officer. Then he was threatened with court-martial...*

New positions were manned in the forest, but there was just a series of strongpoints, nothing that could be called a continuous line. An attack was carried out from these positions, or to be more accurate an attempt was made to carry it out, but nothing was achieved. At that time I was confronted by the Volkssturm for the first time, when I was ordered to lead a weak platoon of old sick men and children up to the positions. I later sent some of them back on my own responsibility, an act that could easily have cost my head..."

The reason why the Red Army did not advance immediately at the Neisse is because they expected to encounter powerful German units and anti-tank weapons in the area of the well-known Neuhammer training camp. In fact, however, there was no such thing present. The OKW announced the Red Army's advance into the area on 11 February 1945:

"In the Breslau—Liegnitz—Glogau area the enemy has advanced to west of Breslau and to the Bober River. Liegnitz fell into enemy hands in the course of fierce fighting."

On 12 February Battle Group Rehfeldt was forced to withdraw from its positions on the Bober opposite Kittlitzstreben. It initially assembled at the Zumm forester's house and then marched in the direction of Tiefenfurt. The Red Army was able to occupy Neuhammer, Halbau, and Striegau simultaneously. About this day the *Wehrmacht* reported euphemistically:

"In Lower Silesia a counterattack by our units frustrated another attempt by the Bolsheviks to sever Fortress Breslau's links with the rear. The enemy lost 60 tanks in a small area south of the city. The battle subsequently extended toward the area around Goldberg, the Queis and the Bober River north of Sagan."

One of the former Hitler Youth members—one of those sent home by the SS officer—remembered the actions in the Tiefenfurt—Klitschdorf area:

"I was born in the mess building of the Neuhammer training camp in 1929. My school days ended in autumn 1944 when I was called up by the Volkssturm. In February 1945 I and five other 15- and 16-year-olds joined Battle Group Rehfeldt. In any case we preferred this to being with old men of 60, for there our comrades were no older than 18 or 19.

On 10 February we left Neuhammer training camp on bicycles and five days later undertook a patrol to Klitschdorf. We then experienced heavy small arms and artillery fire and on the 18th our first assault by Russians screaming their 'Urray!' war cry. Bullets whistled past our ears. On 19 February we carried wounded across an open field, in the process of which some of the wounded were hit again.

From 20 to 25 February we camped in a forest near Niedernenndorf near Rothenburg and moved ammunition and food into the forward positions. Then an SS officer sent us to the rear..."

Actions by SS Battle Group Rehfeldt

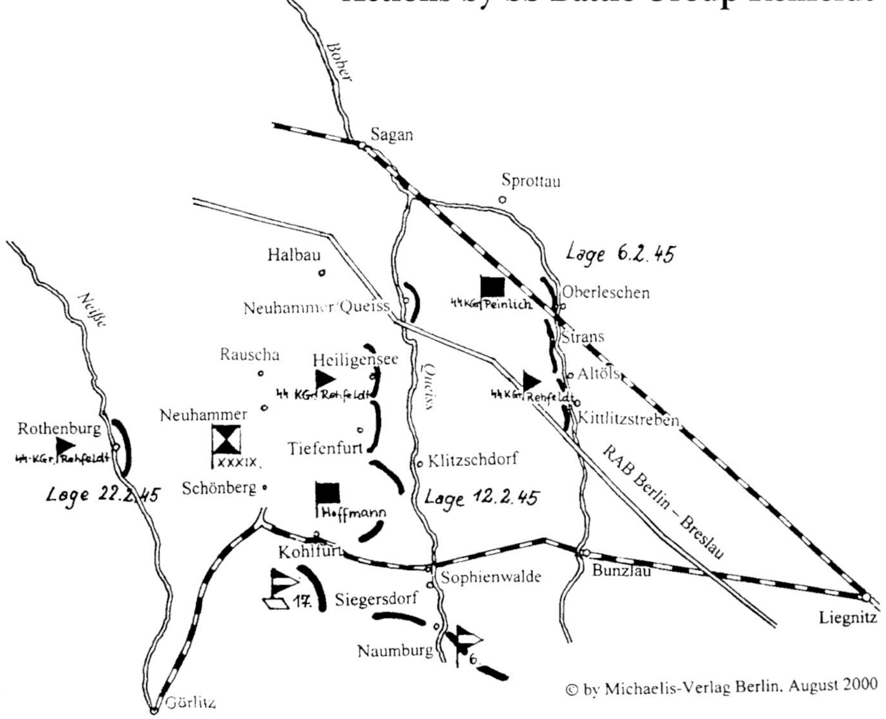

Having fled Neuhammer, on 13 February 1945 SS Battle Group Rehfeldt's command post was located in Heiligensee north of Tiefenfurt. The men took up new defensive positions along the Großen Hammerbach from Heiligensee to Tiefenfurt. Whereas everything had been improvised in the early days of February, it was now possible to attend to administrative matters. Among other things, the Estonian battle group was attached to *Oberst* Hoffmann's regimental group, itself part of Corps Group Friedrich (4th Panzer Army). On 17 February 1945 the battle group occupied a line running Kremsdorf – Neuhammer – Schönberg. In the process *Waffen-Obersturmführer* Georg Iltal was wounded:

"I was born in Estonia in 1918, and in 1937 I joined the military in Reval. There I attended the war academy, from which I was released in 1939 as an officer cadet. After the start of the German-Soviet campaign I initially served in a police unit.

At the end of 1942 I joined the Estonian Legion with the rank of SS-Oberscharführer und SS-Standartenoberjunker. I received officer's training at the Tölz officer school and became the infantry commander's adjutant at the Heidelager training camp. After further training at Amersfort (Holland) I took over the 1st Battery of our artillery as Freiwilligen-Untersturmführer.

In December 1943 I received the Iron Cross, Second Class for my actions at Nevel and in July 1944 the Iron Cross, First Class. Within SS Battle Group Rehfeldt I commanded a company of artillerymen in the fighting in the Neuhammer – Rothenburg area. On 19 February 1945 I was severely wounded by mortar fire at the Neisse River—I took eight splinters in my body and was sent to the reserve hospital in Bad Kissingen..."

Action in Silesia

(February to May 1945)

On 12 January 1945 the Soviets launched their major offensive from the Baranov bridgehead with the objective of reaching the Oder. One week later the OKH informed Army Group A that a battle group from the 20th SS Waffen-Grenadier Division (Estonian No. 1) was to be sent immediately into the area south of Breslau. This consisted of:

the division headquarters
the 45th and 46th SS Waffen-Grenadier Regiments
the 20th SS Anti-Tank Battalion
two battalions of the 20th SS Waffen-Artillery Regiment
supply units

and was attached to the 17th Army. When the enemy unexpectedly crossed the Oder near Borkenheim on 21 January 1945, the 45th SS Waffen-Grenadier Regiment marched straight from the train into the area east of the Soviet bridgehead at Brieg, near Falkenberg. As the commanding officer of the 45th SS Waffen-Grenadier Regiment, *Waffen-Obersturmbannführer* Riipalu, was ill, the commander of the I Battalion, *Waffen-Hauptsturmführer* Maitla, assumed command of the regiment.

SS-Brigadeführer Augsberger immediately decided to counterattack and take the villages of Birkowitz, Halbendorf, and Preisdorf, all outside his assigned sector, in order to cover the northern flank of Fortress Oppeln. The attack was a local success.

The 46th SS Waffen-Grenadier Regiment (*Waffen-Obersturmbannführer* Rebane) did not arrive in the area of operations by rail until 26 January 1945, after which it marched into the Dambrau – Karbischau area. Together with Division Group Hofmann and Harko 312 (Senior Artillery Command 312) if formed the 20th SS Waffen-Grenadier Division's battle group on Corps Group Jeckeln's front.

The Red Army established further bridgeheads on 23-24 January and occupied Oppeln. On 25 January 1945 the *Wehrmacht* reported:

"The enemy attempted to cross the Oder between Gleiwitz and Brieg. He succeeded in taking Oppeln after heavy fighting. Counterattacks smashed most of the attempted crossings of the river. There is still fighting over isolated bridgeheads, which have since been reduced [in size]. Enemy spearheads are approaching Breslau from the southeast. All of the enemy's attacks east of the city failed. A Soviet battle group with 30 tanks crossed the Oder near Steinau but was thrown back after the destruction of 24 tanks."

During the fierce fighting, on 26 January 1945 Police Battle Group Breul reinforced the Estonian division group. When a possible attack from the north into the rear by the Soviet 3rd Guards Army became apparent, the southern elements of the 17th Army (*General der Infanterie* Schulz) withdrew to the Oder. Once again it was too late, for the next day Soviet forces succeeded in encircling numerous units of the 17th Army.

With the withdrawal of troops to the Oder, the commander-in-chief of Army Group A (*Generaloberst* Schörner[76]) abandoned Upper Silesia, almost undamaged and vital to the war effort; however, several badly-battered units escaped certain destruction.

On 3 February 1945 the enemy established a bridgehead near Frohnau and *SS-Brigadeführer und Generalmajor der Waffen-SS* Augsberger organized the defense in Lossen, Johnsdorf, and Jeschen. The next day the enemy launched fierce attacks against the weak forces of Corps Group Jeckeln. The civilian population, still not evacuated and caught by surprise by the attack, faced grim days. In the afternoon, after heavy fighting, the enemy entered Deutsch-Leipe. Near Herzogswalde there was also fierce fighting between troops of the 3rd Guards Army and the 20th SS Waffen-Grenadier Division.

The enemy briefly occupied Grottkau, but troops of the 20th SS Waffen-Grenadier Division and the 45th Volks-Grenadier Division were initially able to drive him out again. Nevertheless, the enemy had forced back the main line of resistance along the Oder to Oppeln, several kilometers to the south. The German units took up defensive positions in the line Oppeln – Grottkau – Wansen.[77] On 9 February 1945 the OKW reported:

> "*North of Ratibor and in the Brieg area, fierce resistance by our troops prevented attempts by the enemy to expand his two bridgeheads and resulted in the destruction of 38 Soviet tanks. The Bolsheviks launched powerful attacks from the Steinau area.*"

After Corps Group Jeckeln was dissolved, on 10 February 1945 Headquarters, VIII Army Corps took over the area and thus the battle group of the 20th SS Waffen-Grenadier Division,[79] which consisted of: three weak and one average battalions of the 45th and 46th SS Waffen-Grenadier Regiments; and six weak and exhausted attached army battalions of Division Group Hofmann.[78]

12 anti-tank guns from the 653rd and 663rd Army Anti-Tank Battalions and four Hetzer tank-destroyers of the 1384th Anti-Tank Company and 248th Anti-Tank Battalion were attached to the 20th SS Anti-Tank Battalion. The artillery was reinforced by a total of 33 guns from various army artillery battalions.[80] The ranks of the SS battle group thus included more army troops than *Waffen-SS* units! On 19 February 1945 the 17th Army was organized as:

- LVII Panzer Corps with:
  - 103rd Panzer Brigade, 8th Panzer Division, and 408th Division
- XXXVIII Army Corps with:
  - 269th Infantry Division, 10th Panzer-Grenadier Division, and 208th Infantry Division

Fortress Breslau with:
fortress garrison and 609th Infantry Division
XVII Panzer Corps with:
19th and 20th Panzer Divisions and 254th Infantry Division
VIII Army Corps with:
100th Light Infantry Division, 45th Volksgrenadier Division, and 20th SS Waffen-Grenadier Division (Estonian No. 1)

On 23 February 1945 *SS-Sturmbannführer* Mützelfeldt, the 1st General Staff Officer, assessed the battle group:

"*No longer suitable for attack because of insufficient infantry strength.*"

The next day the 1st Panzer Army's sector was extended through Cosel to Oppeln, placing the 20th SS Waffen-Grenadier Division under the command of Corps Group Silesia (1st Panzer Army). The corps group—formed from Headquarters, LVI Panzer Corps—was commanded by *General der Kavallerie* Koch-Erpach,[81] and on 1 March 1945 commanded both the 20th SS Waffen-Grenadier Division and the 168th Infantry Division.

On 15 March 1945 the 1st Ukrainian Front took the offensive in the Gross Neukirch (north of Ratibor) area in the direction of Leobschütz and from Grottkau towards the Neisse. The Red Army breached the front in the area of the corps' left boundary as well as that held by the 45th SS Waffen-Grenadier Regiment. Early the next morning Soviet units advancing from the Grottkau area also launched a heavy attack into the Rossdorf – Jatzdorf area. The Alert Regiment Silesia, formed from barely-recuperated patients from the Neisse Reserve Hospital, was destroyed in the fighting. The enemy crossed over to the left bank of the Neisse and rolled toward the city of Neisse. At that time there were no German troops left there. During the movement of the 20th SS Waffen-Grenadier Division's headquarters from Falkenberg to Friedland, the soldiers learned that the enemy had breached the fronts of Corps Group Silesia and XI Army Corps and had linked up in Neustadt. Consequently, the two army corps were encircled in the area of Oberglogau – west of Oppeln – Falkenberg – Friedland.

Still on 17 March 1945 the commanding general of Corps Group Silesia, General Koch-Erpach, decided to break out of the pocket with the battle groups of the 168th Infantry Division and the 20th SS Waffen-Grenadier Division toward Neustadt in the direction of the Altvater Mountains. In preparation for the attack *SS-Brigadeführer und Generalmajor der Waffen-SS* Augsberger organized his troops into three groups. The first he commanded personally, while the second was led by *SS-Hauptsturmführer* Langhorst[82] and the third was commanded by *Waffen-Obersturmbannführer* Rebane. The 45th and 46th SS Waffen-Grenadier Regiments initially held their positions north of Falkenberg. After the Red Army had already occupied Neustadt, the breakout attempt failed, and Augsberger and his adjutant *SS-Obersturmführer* Hinz were killed. Those that could join up with the remnants of the 344th Infantry Division and the 18th SS Volunteer Panzer-Grenadier Division under the command of *Generalmajor* Jolasse in the direction of Deutsch-Rasselwitz—Hotzenplotz. Heinrich Beck (20th SS Signals Battalion) described the breakout in a letter to the father of a fallen comrade:

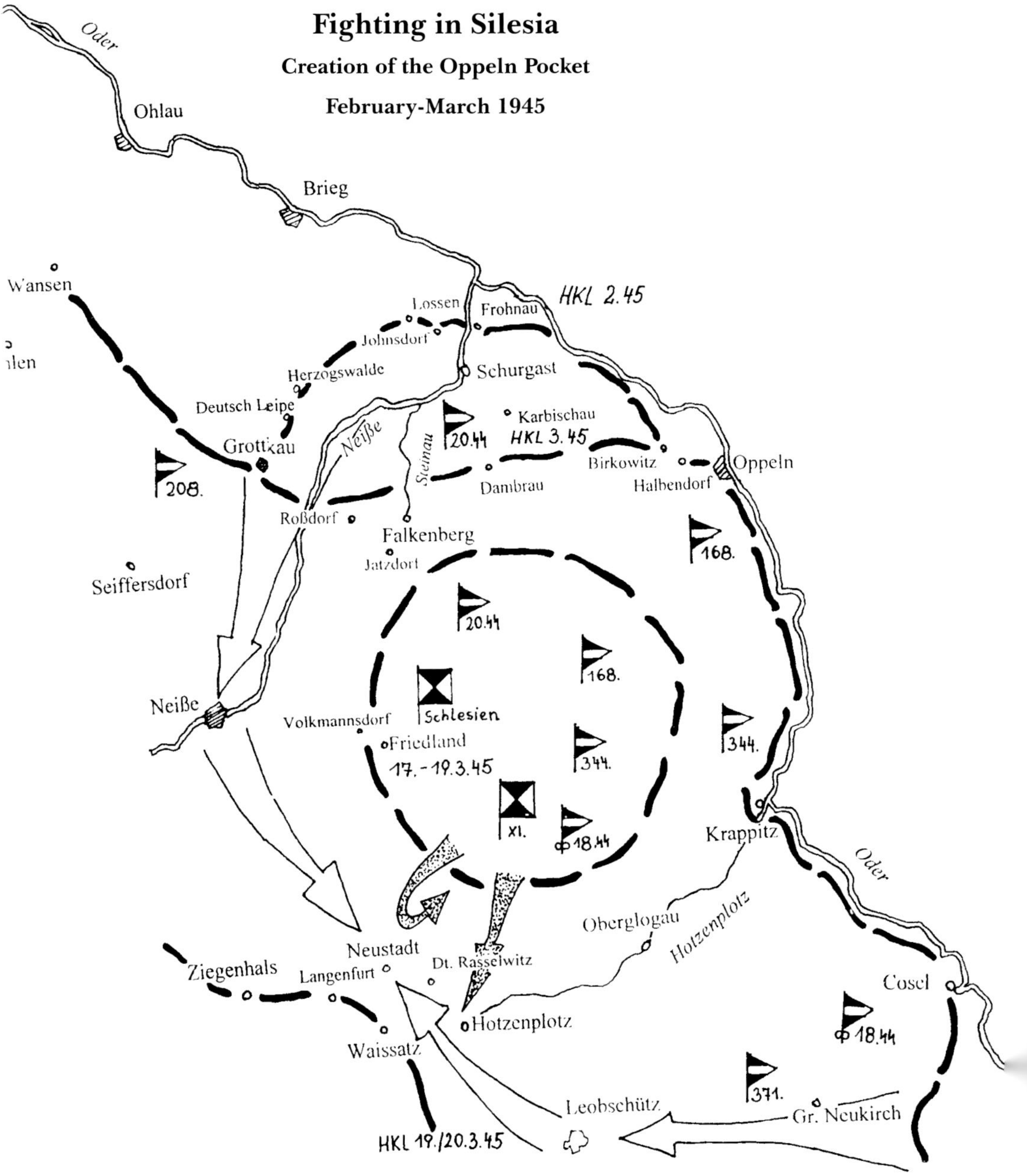
Fighting in Silesia
Creation of the Oppeln Pocket
February-March 1945
Oder
Ohlau
Brieg
Wansen
HKL 2.45
Lossen
Frohnau
Johnsdorf
Herzogswalde
Schurgast
Deutsch Leipe
Karbischau
Grottkau
Neiße
Steinau
20.44
HKL 3.45
208.
Birkowitz
Oppeln
Dambrau
Halbendorf
Roßdorf
Falkenberg
Jatzdorf
168.
Seiffersdorf
20.44
168.
Neiße
Schlesien
344.
Volkmannsdorf
Friedland
17.-19.3.45
344.
XI.
18.44
Krappitz
Oder
Oberglogau
Hotzenplotz
Neustadt
Dt. Rasselwitz
Ziegenhals
Langenfurt
Cosel
Hotzenplotz
Waissatz
18.44
371.
Leobschütz
Gr. Neukirch
HKL 19./20.3.45

"My dear Herr Peters,

I must now keep a promise that Gustav and I made to each other a year ago. Your son—my comrade—met a soldier's death during the breakout from the pocket near Neisse. I want to describe to you the circumstances.

We received orders to break through to the German lines during the night at all costs. Gustav led the foot elements of the 1st Company, I led my own company, which was part of the same battalion. We were led by our division commander SS-Brigadeführer Augsberger. Gustav and I stayed close together so as to be able to help one another if the need arose. During the darkness all went well and there was no enemy contact. At daybreak we were nearing the German lines, but there was still a thin line of Soviet infantry in front of us.

After hasty preparations in a wood we stormed the Russian positions, which were abandoned almost without a fight. Two Russian tanks had appeared in the meantime, however, and after about five minutes they were reinforced by a third T-34, an anti-tank gun and heavy artillery. We had to cross an open field about four kilometers wide east and west of the village of Volkmannsdorf (approx. 35 km NW of Leobschütz). The T-34s had positioned themselves on a ridge on its southern edge and together with the anti-tank gun and artillery poured heavy fire onto us. As we had no heavy weapons, and with no available cover, countermeasures were out of the question.

We had passed Volkmannsdorf and cleared it of the enemy. Gustav was 10 to 12 paces behind me. Gustav was killed halfway between Volkmannsdorf and the wood due west of the village. Suddenly, from behind me I heard my name called. I turned round and saw Gustav lying face-down. I immediately crawled back to him, called Gustav by name and shook him. When he didn't answer I turned him over and saw that he had been hit in the chest. The hole had been made by a shell fragment. It was about the size of a pea and was a finger's width to the right of his left nipple. Gustav had only been able to call out my name and then died. I then tried to slip his ring from his finger, but it was on too tight. Gustav had nothing else on him as we had left everything in the pocket.

I was then forced to turn my attention back to my company, which by then was far ahead. We were unable to bury Gustav as we were in the midst of the enemy lines. We also had to leave our general, who was killed about 200 meters from Gustav."

At dusk on 19 March 1945 the encircled troops tried to break out across muddy, trackless fields to Deutsch-Rasselwitz. The barren terrain lay under heavy artillery and mortar fire. The soldiers, who were accompanied by many civilians (women, children, and old men), took the town and advanced to the Hotzenplotz und Braune. The bridges over the river had already been destroyed, however, and the last vehicles, artillery, and assault guns had to be abandoned.

As the division headquarters and the individual units had lost all communication with upper echelon, LVI Panzer Corps initially thought the SS unit destroyed. Then the headquarters arrived at the division's assembly point at Ziegenhals under the command of *SS-Obersturmbannführer* Mützelfeldt, the operations officer, three days later on 22 March 1945. That same evening the remnants of the division were ordered into the Bolkenhain area, about 30 km to the south, to be VIII Army Corps' reserve. By way of Waldenburg the exhausted and battle-weary men finally reached Ketzdorf, near Hirschberg. There they were able to rest and were issued new equipment.

The division was brought to Hitler's attention at the daily situation briefing on 23 March 1945 when, following LVI Panzer Corps' report on the 20th SS Waffen-Grenadier Division, General Burgdorf[83] declared:

"*Yes, the Estonians left immediately. One must also imagine it psychologically. A little much was demanded of them.*"

Hitler: "*What are they fighting for anyway? They are away from home.*"

Burgdorf: "*If we already have a large number of fainthearted people, it really is impossible to demand much of them.*"

In the war diary appendix on 23 March 1945, the General Staff of the Army/ Operations Department I wrote of the 20th SS Waffen-Grenadier Division's remaining strength:

"*A tossed-together grenadier regiment with 500-600 men and 50 machine-guns plus 200 artillerymen without weapons. There is also a pioneer company with 30 men and a tank-destroyer!*"

This was, however, just the first report about the men turning up in the assembly area. Others had also escaped the pocket and were in other areas or attached to other units, out of contact with unit headquarters. Several groups were also behind the Soviet lines, trying to make it back to the German main line of resistance. The former *Waffen-Untersturmführer* Feliks Tamm was captured by the Soviets in March 1945:

"*I was born in 1919 and in 1939-40 graduated from the war academy as an officer candidate. I served as an enlisted man until discharged in the summer of 1940. From then on I worked as janitor. I and several other young men hid out when the Soviets pulled out in 1941 and deported many laborers.*

General mobilization was declared in Estonia in February 1944. I was drafted and came to the 20th SS Volunteer Division. As I had been in the artillery in the Estonian Army, I was sent to the 20th SS Volunteer Artillery Regiment. I took part in the fighting at the Narva and like many other members of the division eventually ended up in Neuhammer. There I was ordered to attend a course in Beneschau. I participated in the fighting at the Oder as a Waffen-Untersturmführer. Our guns were spiked there and we artillerymen were used as infantry. At the end of March 1945 I was captured by the Soviets.

The commander of a T-34 asked me if I was an officer, to which I replied that I was. He pulled out a bottle of vodka and we drank together. The next day he advised me to take off my uniform, as I might be shot otherwise. I followed his advice, nevertheless I was sent to Siberia for ten years. But I survived..."

At the end of March *SS-Oberführer* Maack took over the remnants of the division in place of the fallen *SS-Brigadeführer* Augsberger. A revision of the negative opinion previously held by senior officers became apparent when the division was attached to VIII Army Corps (17th Army) on 15 April 1945.[84] The corps consisted of:

- the 208th Infantry Division
- the 100th Light Infantry Division
- the 17th Infantry Division
- the remnants of the 20th SS Waffen-Grenadier Division

The division marched from Bolkenhain through Schönau to the front south of Goldberg, the latter having already been occupied by Soviet troops. The 45th SS Waffen-Grenadier Regiment occupied the left wing facing Neukirch and the 47th SS Waffen-Grenadier Regiment the right wing. There the division received reinforcements in the shape of the 20th SS Pioneer Battalion formed in Dresden under *Waffen-Hauptsturmführer* Telliskivi and two police companies. Action in the days that followed was limited to patrolling by both sides and Soviet artillery and mortar fire. This caused few casualties, however, for the positions, which had been taken over from the *Wehrmacht*, were well-built and were even protected by minefields. Nevertheless, the 20th SS Pioneer Battalion immediately began constructing additional positions.

On 21 April 1945 *SS-Brigadeführer* Maack visited the individual units in the main line of resistance. There was no further heavy fighting. When news of the imminent surrender was released, the entire Silesian front began pulling back to the west. In some cases this resulted in incidents that could not be overlooked. A former member recalled:

"At dusk the order came for the men to climb aboard passing vehicles. The battalion had no vehicles of its own any more and most of the Wehrmacht vehicles coming from various directions were fully loaded. In most cases only single men were able to climb onto one and the same vehicle. Under such conditions command of units was completely lost. The retreat lasted the whole night and because of the load was very slow.

An interesting rumor went around to the effect that our Knight's Cross wearer Rebane had spoken with an American and a Czech general about sending our division back.

At noon our regimental commander Waffen-Sturmbannführer Maitla stood beside his vehicle at a crossroads and personally directed the oncoming vehicles in the direction of Jungbunzlau. He was self-confident and in good spirits..."

After the remnants of the division marched through Reichenberg – Turnau into the area around Melnik, they tried to reach the German border near Annaberg. There the last surrendered to the Soviets. Only a few succeeded in making their way through to the western allies. Former *SS-Oberfunker* Arved Alupere recalled the fighting in Silesia:

"I was born in the Tartu District on 3 November 1926. During my student years I was a member of the "Young Eagles", an Estonian youth organization to which almost every schoolboy belonged.

In January 1942 at the age of 15 I joined the self-defense force, as I was too young for the other units. The self-defense force helped keep the supply routes open, guarded prisoners of war and was used to defend objects (e.g. bridges). Later I fought near Lake Peipus as a member of the self-defense force attached to a German anti-partisan group.

Then on 17 August 1944 I joined the Waffen-SS. In the self-defense force the units of the Waffen-SS had always been our examples. We wanted to fight like them. I came to the 20th SS Waffen-Grenadier Division as a trained radio operator and was attached to the headquarters of II Battalion, 46th SS Waffen-Grenadier Regiment.

When we pulled out of Estonia several weeks later, it hit us hard. No one wanted to leave his homeland. Many cried as they stood at the railings of the ships taking them to Germany. When we were transferred from Neuhammer to the vicinity of Oppeln, we took Karbischau and defended our positions there for more than two months. The Soviets attacked with tanks and heavy artillery almost every day. The battalion headquarters (SS-Hauptsturmführer Licht) was in Karbischau, in a castle 200 meters from the front.

When we were finally encircled in the Oppeln Pocket, we fought for seven days until we were able to break out. I received six small shell splinters in my arm during the fighting. After the breakout I was promoted to Oberfunker and was awarded the Close Combat Clasp. On 9 May 1945 I was captured in Czechoslovakia and I experienced all the terrors that went with it."

Thus, after 2½ years ended the tragic story of the soldiers of a small nation who served in the *Waffen-SS*. Altogether, about 35,000 Estonians served in the 20th SS Waffen-Grenadier Division (Estonian No. 1). The percentage of volunteers was relatively small. Even during its establishment there were many secondments from the police battalions. The same happened when Estonia declared general mobilization in February 1944, when many were called up by the *Waffen-SS* and were incorporated into the division as complete units (e.g. Eastern Battalions) shortly before the Soviet summer offensive. The last elements—including the Self-Defense Force)—were transferred to the ranks of the *Waffen-SS* at Neuhammer in October 1944.

In the struggle for their homeland most were highly motivated, and Estonian SS battle groups proved themselves often. As the units of the 20th SS Waffen-Grenadier Division (Estonian No. 1) were almost always committed apart from each other in Estonia, the role of division commander Augsberger was largely administrative.

In the summer of 1944, however, inadequate training, shortages of weapons, and command errors—especially by *Waffen-Standartenführer* Tuuling of the 46th SS Waffen-Grenadier Regiment—led to heavy casualties. When it was announced that the *Wehrmacht* was leaving Estonia in late summer 1944, thousands of Estonians deserted. Many tried to continue the struggle against the Soviets as partisans. Far from home and with no hope of a German victory, those who were part of the reestablishment of the division at Neuhammer in October 1944 lacked motivation. While some Estonian units (such as SS Border Police Regiments) were simply incorporated into the Red Army when captured and fought against German troops, the members of the 20th SS Waffen-Grenadier Division (Estonian No. 1) were all given long prison sentences, most of which were served in Siberian labor camps. Most of these prisoners of war did not return home for 10 years.

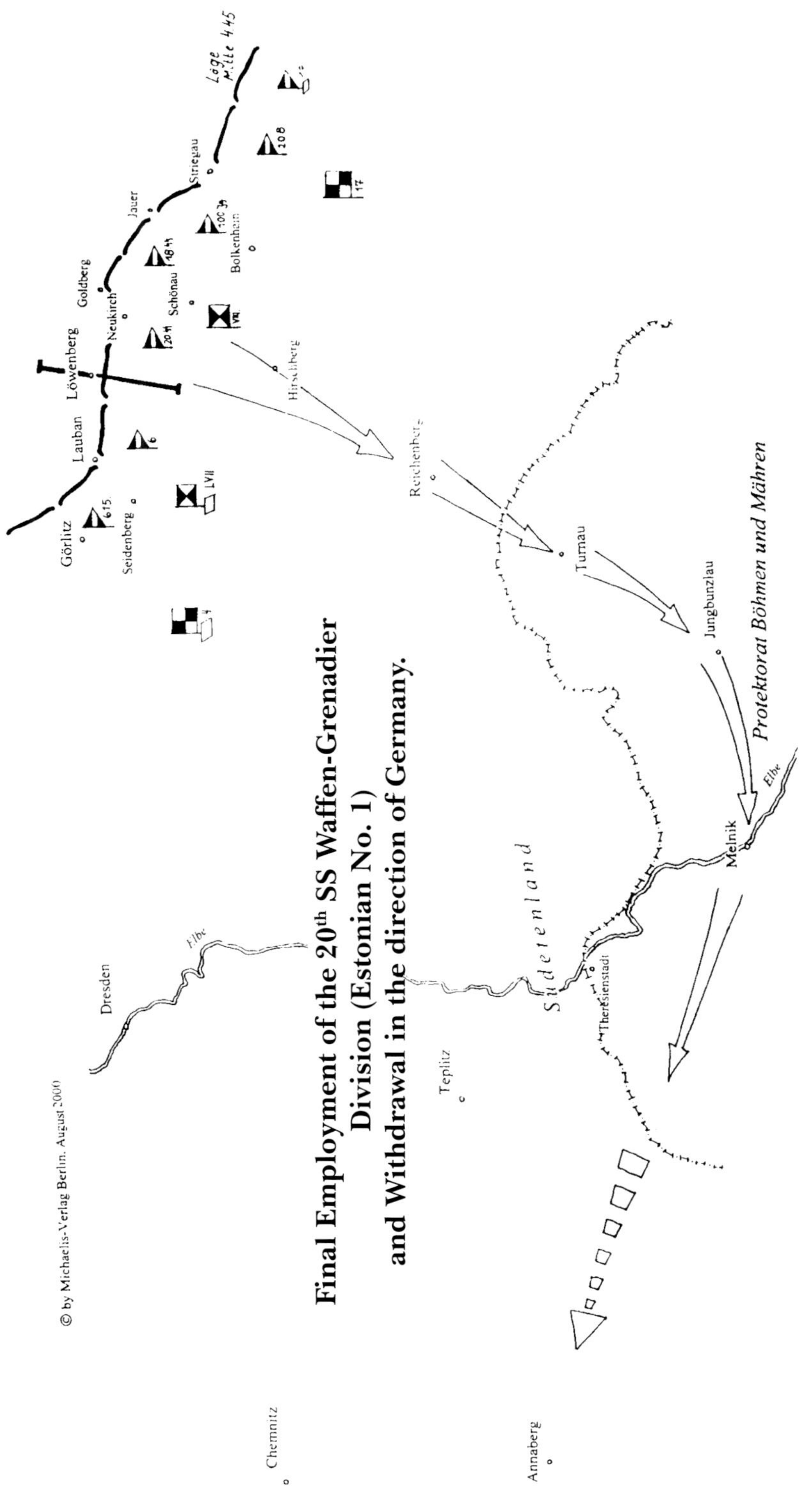

Final Employment of the 20th SS Waffen-Grenadier Division (Estonian No. 1) and Withdrawal in the direction of Germany.

Wilhelm Barenscheer

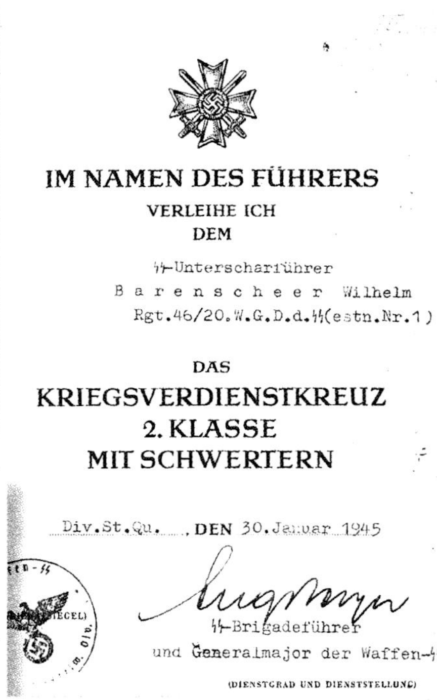

IM NAMEN DES FÜHRERS

VERLEIHE ICH

DEM

ϟϟ-Unterscharführer

B a r e n s c h e e r Wilhelm

Rgt.46/20.W.G.D.d.ϟϟ(estn.Nr.1)

DAS

KRIEGSVERDIENSTKREUZ

2. KLASSE

MIT SCHWERTERN

Div.St.Qu., DEN 30.Januar 1945

ϟϟ-Brigadeführer

und Generalmajor der Waffen-ϟϟ

(DIENSTGRAD UND DIENSTSTELLUNG)

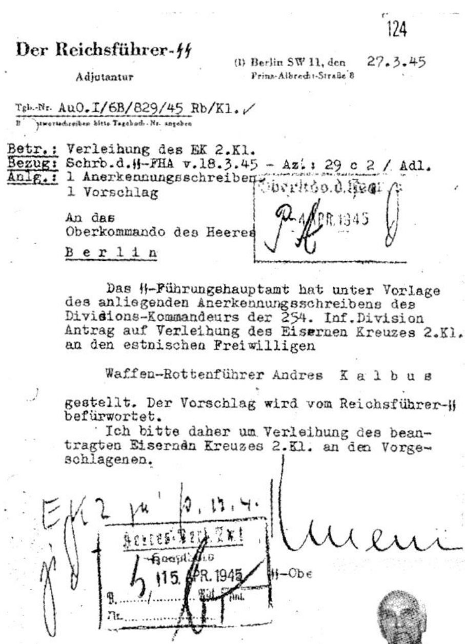

124

Der Reichsführer-ϟϟ

Adjutantur

Berlin SW 11, den 27.3.45

Prinz-Albrecht-Straße 8

Tgb.-Nr. AuO.I/6B/829/45 Rb/Kl.

Betr.: Verleihung des EK 2.Kl.

Bezug: Schrb.d.ϟϟ-FHA v.18.3.45 - Az.: 29 c 2 / Adl.

Anlg.: 1 Anerkennungsschreiben

1 Vorschlag

An das

Oberkommando des Heeres

B e r l i n

Das ϟϟ-Führungshauptamt hat unter Vorlage des anliegenden Anerkennungsschreibens des Divisions-Kommandeurs der 254. Inf.Division Antrag auf Verleihung des Eisernen Kreuzes 2.Kl. an den estnischen Freiwilligen

Waffen-Rottenführer Andres K a l b u s

gestellt. Der Vorschlag wird vom Reichsführer-ϟϟ befürwortet.

Ich bitte daher um Verleihung des beantragten Eisernen Kreuzes 2.Kl. an den Vorgeschlagenen.

ϟϟ-Obe

Three Estonian Knight's Cross wearers from l. to r.: *Waffen-Obersturmbannführer* Rebane, *Waffen-Unterscharführer* Nugiseks, and *Waffen-Obersturmbannführer* Riipalu.

Harald Nugiseks and the author

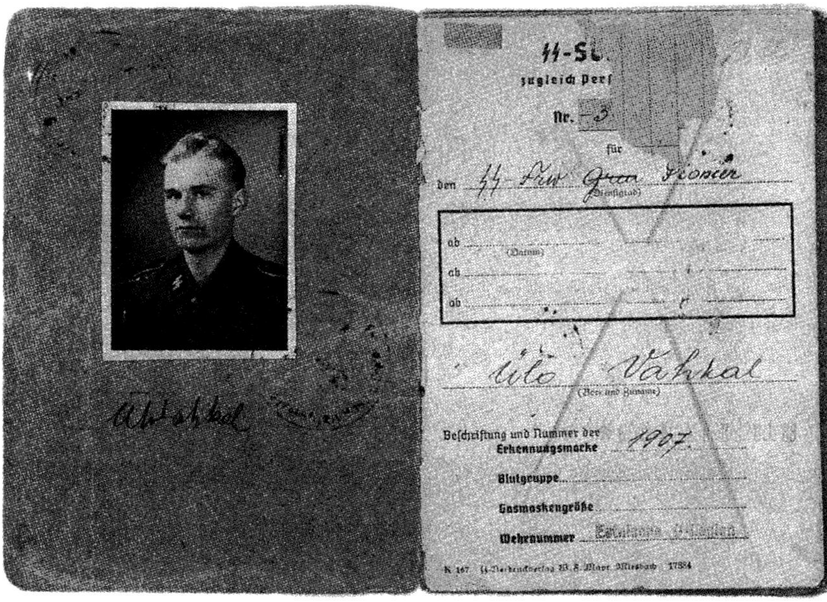

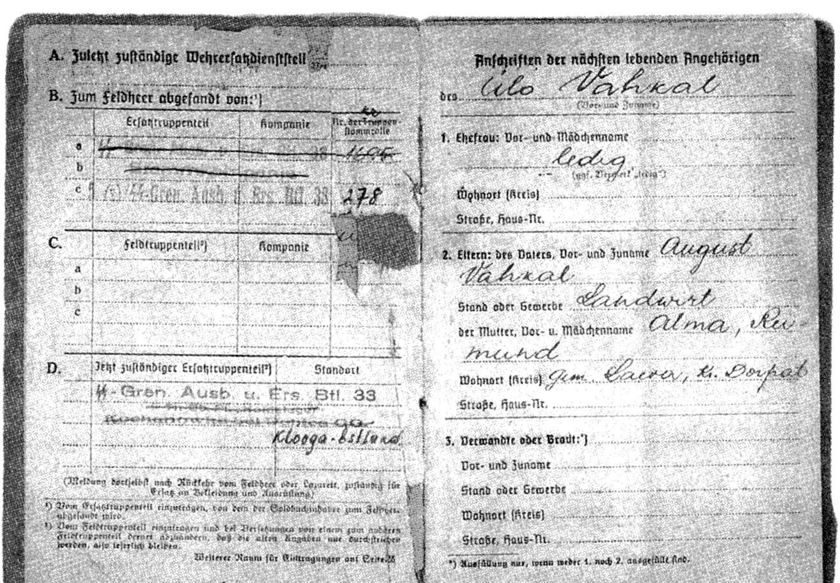

Ülo Vahkal's paybook.

Appendices

Appendix 1

Chronology

01/10/1942 – 03/1943	Formation of the Estonian Legion in Debica
23/03/1943 – 03/1944 SS	Panzer-Grenadier Battalion Narva in action with the SS Panzer-Grenadier Division Wiking
03/1943 – 29/10/1943	Formation of the 3rd Estonian SS Volunteer Brigade
01/11/1943 – 10/11/1943	"Operation Heinrich" in the Polotsk – Krasnopolye – Pustoshka – Idritsa – Sebesh area
24/01/1944	Order for expansion into the 20thES SS Volunteer Division
15/02/1944 – 19/02/1944	I./45th SS Volunteer Grenadier Regiment in action
10/02/1944 – 24/09/1944	Employment of the division in Estonia
20/04/1944	Incorporation of Estonian Eastern Battalions 658, 659, 660
14/08/1944 – 24/08/1944	SS Battle Group Rebane in action in Tartu area
14/08/1944 – 08/09/1944	SS Battle Group Wagner in action in Tartu area
15/10/1944 – 31/01/1945	SS Battle Group Rehfeldt in action between the Bober and Neisse Rivers
06/02/1945 – 28/02/1945	SS Battle Group Rehfeldt in action between the Bober and Neisse Rivers
21/01/1945 – 19/03/1945	Fighting in Silesia and the Oppeln Pocket
22/03/1945 – 15/04/1945	Division rested and brought up to strength in the Bolkenhain area
16/04/1945 – 09/05/1945	Action at the front near Goldberg, Silesia

Appendix 2

Wearers of the Knight's Cross of the Iron Cross

SS-Brigadeführer Franz Augsberger		31 March 1945
SS-Sturmbannführer Georg Eberhardt		04 August 1943
SS-Hauptsturmführer Bernhard Langhorst		05 April 1945
Waffen-Hauptsturmführer Paul Maitla		23 August 1944
Freiwilligen-Unterscharführer Harald Nugiseks		09 April 1944
Freiwilligen-Standartenführer Alfons Rebane	Knight's Cross Oak Leaves	23 February1944 09 May 1945
Waffen-Obersturmbannführer Harald Riipalu		23 August 1944

Appendix 3

Military Postal Numbers and Command Positions

Division Headquarters	M.P.N. 59 340	*SS-Brigadeführer* Franz Augsberger
		SS-Oberführer Maack
I a		*SS-Sturmbannführer* Hans-J. Mützelfeldt
I b		*SS-Hauptsturmführer* Rudolf Bösel
I c		*SS-Sturmbannführer* Willy Krüger
II a		*SS-Obersturmführer* Willy Kießling
IV a		*SS-Sturmbannführer* Emil Talbot von
Pistor IV b		*SS-Sturmbannführer* Walter Pfitzner

45th SS Waffen-Grenadier Regiment (Estonian No. 1)

Headquarters	M.P.N. 48 001	*Freiw-Obersturmbannführer* Paul Vent
		Waffen-Obersturmbannführer H. Riipalu
I Battalion	M.P.N. 56 475	*Freiw-Sturmbannführer* Harald Riipalu
		Waffen-Hauptsturmführer Paul Maitla
		Waffen-Hauptsturmführer Elmar Lipping
II Battalion	M.P.N. 48 958	*SS-Sturmbannführer* Elmar Lang
		Freiw.-Hauptsturmführer Ludvig Triik
		Waffen-Hauptsturmführer Erich Palk
III Battalion	M.P.N. 13 803	
IV Battalion	M.P.N. 56 475	
16th Company	M.P.N. 58 312	
17th Company	M.P.N. 48 052	
18th Company	M.P.N. 48 775	

46th SS Waffen-Grenadier Regiment (Estonian No. 2)

Headquarters	M.P.N. 36 341	*Freiw.-Standartenführer* Juhan Tuuling
		Waffen-Sturmbannführer Alfons Rebane
I Battalion	M.P.N. 39 340	*Freiw.-Sturmbannführer* Ain-Ervin Mere
		Waffen-Hauptsturmführer Jaan Sepa
		Waffen-Sturmbannführer Theo Liht
		Waffen-Hauptsturmführer Valdur Jürissaar
II Battalion	M.P.N. 38 304	*Freiw.-Sturmbannführer* Udo Parrest
		Freiw.-Hauptsturmführer Rudolf Bruus
		Freiw.-Hauptsturmführer Werner Müthel
		Waffen-Sturmbannführer Friedrich Kurg
III Battalion		M.P.N. 15 973

47th SS Waffen-Grenadier Regiment (Estonian No. 3)

Headquarters	M.P.N. 22 166	*Waffen-Obersturmbannführer* Paul Vent
		Waffen-Obersturmbannführer Juhan Vermet
		SS-Obersturmbannführer Hans Belzer
I Battalion	M.P.N. 16 836	*Waffen-Sturmbannführer* Georg Sooden
II Battalion	M.P.N. 25 712	*Freiw.-Sturmbannführer* Alfons Rebane
		Waffen-Hauptsturmführer Jaan Sepa
III Battalion	M.P.N. 24 586	*Waffen-Hauptsturmführer* Eduard Hints

20th SS Waffen-Artillery Regiment (Estonian No. 1)

Headquarters	M.P.N. 48 052	*Freiw.-Obersturmbannführer* Aleksander Sobolev
		Waffen-Sturmbannführer August V
I Battalion	M.P.N. 09 046	*Freiw.-Sturmbannführer* August Vöhma
		Waffen-Hauptsturmführer Aleksander Kimmel
II Battalion	M.P.N. 27 051	*SS-Sturmbannführer* Richard Rubach
		Freiw.-Hauptsturmführer Nigul Maanemaa
III Battalion	M.P.N. 18 194	*Freiw.-Hauptsturmführer* Priit Eras
IV Battalion	M.P.N. 28 668	*Freiw.-Sturmbannführer* Paul Suurkivi

20th SS Fusilier Battalion

Headquarters	M.P.N. 48 314	*SS-Hauptsturmführer* Wallner
		SS-Obersturmführer Hans Jäger
		Waffen-Obersturmführer Hando Ruus
1st Company		*Waffen-Obersturmbannführer* Oskar Ruut
2nd Company		*Freiw.-Hauptsturmführer* Hugo Siim
3rd Company		*Freiw.-Untersturmführer* Hando Ruus
4th Company		*Waffen-Hauptsturmführer* Oskar Puusepp

20th SS Pioneer Battalion

Headquarters	M.P.N. 23 417	*SS-Hauptsturmführer* Willy Peetz
		Waffen-Hauptsturmführer Robert Telliskivi
1st Company	M.P.N. 48 775	*Waffen-Obersturmführer* Lembit Juhari
2nd Company	M.P.N. 58 312	*Waffen-Obersturmführer* Elmar Otsing
3rd Company	M.P.N. 26 985	*Waffen-Obersturmführer* Robert Telliskivi

20th SS Signals Battalion

Headquarters	M.P.N. 17 403	*SS-Sturmbannführer* Arno Grohmann
1st Company	M.P.N. 31 139	
2nd Company	M.P.N. 56 819	

20th SS Supply Units

Headquarters	M.P.N. 19 766	*Freiw.-Hauptsturmführer* Tammekand
		SS-Sturmbannführer Willi Krüger
1st Bicycle Troop	M.P.N. 36 356	
2nd Bicycle Troop	M.P.N. 30 539	
Supply Company	M.P.N. 21 252	
Vehicle Repair Platoon	M.P.N. 29 253	
Workshop Company	M.P.N. 56 464	

20th SS Medical Battalion

Commanding Officer		*SS-Sturmbannführer* Dr. Walter Pfitzner
1st Company	M.P.N. 17 113	
2nd Company	M.P.N. 20 794	
Decontamination Platoon	M.P.N. 17 113	
Medical Supply Company	M.P.N. 29 253	
Ambulance Platoon	M.P.N. 46 085	
20th SS Economic Battalion	M.P.N. 06 930	

20th SS Waffen Training and Replacement Regiment

		SS-Sturmbannführer Georg Ahlemann[85]
		SS-Obersturmbannführer Emil Rehfeldt
I Battalion		*Waffen-Hauptsturmführer* Theodor Liht
		Waffen-Hauptsturmführer Ludvig Triik
II Battalion		*Waffen-Hauptsturmführer* Ludvig Triik
		Waffen-Hauptsturmführer Riho Piirsalu
		Waffen-Hauptsturmführer Erich Palk
		Waffen-Sturmbannführer Hendrik Sillapere
20th SS Field Replacement Battalion	M.P.N. 38 087	*SS-Hauptsturmführer* Fritz Störtz
20th SS Flak Battalion	M.P.N. 01 199	*SS-Hauptsturmführer* Fritz Bergemann
20th SS Anti-Tank Battalion	M.P.N. 48 886	*SS-Hauptsturmführer* Bernhard Langhorst
20th SS Field Post Office	M.P.N. 05 430	*SS-Obersturmführer* Werner Lundt

Appendix 4
Short Biographies

Georg Ahlemann was born in Havelberg on 15 January 1911. He joined the NSDAP (No. 124,829) and its *Schutzstaffel* (No. 50,686). He served as a guard at the Dachau concentration camp in 1937-38, and in 1939 he took part in the formation of the reinforced *SS-Totenkopf Standarten*. In SS-Division *Nord*, formed from SS Battle Group *Nord*, he commanded the SS Reconnaissance Battalion in Karelia as a *SS-Hauptsturmführer* until assigned to the Estonian SS Legion. Promoted to *SS-Sturmbannführer* on 9 November 1943, until October 1944 Ahlemann led the 20th SS Waffen-Grenadier Training and Replacement Regiment.

Franz Augsberger was born in Vienna on 10 October 1905 and trained as an engineer. In 1927 he joined the Home Defense Force, and in October 1930 became a member of the NSDAP and the SA. On 20 April 1932 he moved from the SA to the SS (No. 139,528). Augsberger was active politically as a district speaker and propaganda leader. In 1933, after the NSDAP was banned in Austria, he left the country and moved to Germany. In October 1934 the armed SS (*SS-Verfügungstruppe*) took him in as a platoon commander. After attending the SS Officer School in Brunswick, on 1 June 1935 Augsberger was promoted to *SS-Untersturmführer*. He was initially assigned to the Central Office for Race and Resettlement,[86] and in May 1936 he began serving as an instructor in ideology at the SS Officer School in Brunswick. On 30 January 1939, by then a *SS-Hauptsturmführer*, he was transferred to the replacement *Sturmbann* of the *SS-Standarte "Der Führer,"* and on 1 August 1940 to the *SS-Regiment (mot.) "Westland."* Promoted to *SS-Sturmbannführer* on 1 August 1939, he commanded a battalion in SS-Infanterie-Regiment 7 and as an *SS-Obersturmbannführer* (20 April 1942) was awarded the German Cross in Gold on 20 May 1942. In February 1943 he took over the Estonian SS Legion. Following promotion to *SS-Standartenführer* (1 July 1943) and *SS-Oberführer*, on 21 June 1944 he achieved the rank of *SS-Brigadeführer und Generalmajor der Waffen-SS*. He thus became the first graduate of the Brunswick SS Officer School to attain the rank of *General der Waffen-SS*. Awarded the Knight's Cross on 8 March 1945, Augsberger was killed on 17 March 1945 in Silesia as commander of the 20th SS Waffen-Grenadier Division (Estonian No. 1). Leo Sipelgas served in the division headquarters from 1944 and recalled of Augsberger:

"*Franz Augsberger was a man with a sense of humor, whose friendly nature enabled him to get along with almost everyone. In many crisis situations, however, he quickly lost his head—for example in the Blue Mountains or during the retreat from Estonia. Rebane or Riipalu often had to take command. They did this just as well!*"

[86] This was in keeping with Himmler's wish that every graduate from an officer school should serve as a platoon commander in the SS-Verfügungstruppe for 10 months, followed by 10 months in the Central Office for Race and Resettlement for ideological training. Usually the officer then had to serve 10 months in the SD as well. Following this the man was assigned to a unit or to one of the numerous SS offices.

Erich von dem Bach (-Zelewski) was born in Lauenburg on 1 March 1889. He fought in the First World War and was decorated with the Iron Crosses, First and Second Class. In 1919 he served in the Eastern Border Guard and Upper Silesia. He left the service in 1924 as a *Leutnant*. In 1930 he joined the NSDAP, and one year later the SS (No. 9,831). On 15 December 1934 Bach attained the rank of an *SS-Gruppenführer* and became SS Senior Sector Commander "Northeast" (East Prussia). After conflicts with *Gauleiter* Koch he was relieved, and on 15 February 1936 took over Senior Sector "Southeast" (Silesia). On 28 June 1938 he was named Senior SS and Police Commander "Southeast." On 10 April 1941 he received the supplementary rank of *Generalleutnant der Polizei*. Three weeks later Bach was transferred to the personal staff of the *Reichsführer-SS*, and on 22 June 1941 became Senior SS and Police Commander "Central Russia." Effective 9 November 1941 he was promoted to the rank of *SS-Obergruppenführer und General der Polizei*. Having been named Commissioner of the *Reichsführer-SS* for Anti-Bandit Operations on 23 October 1942, on 21 June 1943 he was placed in command of all anti-bandit units. From 1 July 1944 he was permitted to bear the title of *General der Waffen-SS*. After the retreat from White Russia, from August to mid-October 1944 he led Corps Group von dem Bach, which was responsible for suppressing the Warsaw uprising. On 30 September 1944 he was awarded the Knight's Cross of the Iron Cross for his actions. From 10 November 1944 until 25 January 1945 Bach commanded the corps headquarters of XIV SS Army Corps, which was deployed on the Upper Rhine. From 26 January to 10 February 1945 the command of X SS Army Corps assembled in Posen-West Prussia. One week later he took over the so-called "Oder Corps." Bach was held prisoner by the Allies until 1950, and at the Nuremberg Trials he testified against the principal war criminals as a witness for the prosecution. Not until 1961 was he sentenced to 4½ years in prison for manslaughter. One year later he was given life imprisonment for multiple murders. He died in prison on 8 March 1972.

Gottlob Berger was born in Gerstetten on 16 July 1896. He served as a volunteer in the First World War, and his last position was as *Leutnant* Adjutant of III./I.R. 476. He was demobilized on 5 February 1920. Two years later, while working as a seminary teacher, Berger joined the Nazi Party. Active in the SA since 1930, on 30 January 1936 he was taken into the SS with the rank of *SS-Oberführer*. On 20 April 1939, with the rank of *SS-Brigadeführer*, he took over the *SS-Ergänzungsamt*. After two years he became head of the *SS-Hauptamt* with the rank of *SS-Gruppenführer*. Promotion to *SS-Obergruppenführer und General der Waffen-SS* followed on 21 June 1943. In addition to functioning as head of the SS-FHA, he was also State Secretary in the Reich Ministry for the Occupied Eastern Territories (Rosenberg). During the attempt to put down the Slovakian National Uprising in 1944 Berger showed himself to be unfit for the task, and was relieved after a few days. For his efforts to expand the *Waffen-SS*, on 15 November 1944 he was awarded the Knight's Cross of the War Merit Cross with Swords. He died in his home town on 5 January 1975.

Rudolf von Bünau was born in Stuttgart on 19 August 1890, and on 15 July 1909 began his military life as an officer cadet. On 16 November 1910 he was promoted to *Leutnant* in Grenadier Regiment 119. After the First World War and the *Reichswehr*, Bünau, an *Oberst* since 1 August 1936, became commander of Infantry Regiment 133. Two months after his promotion to *Generalmajor*, on 1 November 1940 he took over the 177th Infantry Division. Eight weeks after his promotion to *Generalleutnant* on 1 September 1942 he assumed command of the 73rd Infantry Division. On 1 November 1943 he was placed in command of XXXXVII Panzer Corps. After a brief period as commander of LII Army Corps, on 1 April 1944 von Bünau was named commanding general of XI Army Corps. On 1 April 1944 he was promoted to *General der Infanterie*. Decorated with the Knight's Cross with Oak Leaves, in April 1945 von Bünau served as commander of the Vienna Defense District and commander of Corps von Bünau.

Wilhelm Burgdorf was born in Fürstenwalde on 15 February 1895. He joined the 12th Grenadier Regiment as an officer candidate on 1 August 1914, and on 18 April was promoted to *Leutnant*. After serving in the *Reichswehr*, on 1 October 1937 he became adjutant in the IX Army Corps. After promotion to *Oberstleutnant* on 1 August 1938, in summer 1940 he took over the 529th Infantry Regiment. In that post he was promoted to *Oberst* on 1 September 1940 and received the Knight's Cross on 29 September 1941. He became a department head in the Army Personnel Office on 1 May 1942, and on 1 October 1942 he was promoted to *Generalmajor* and made deputy head of the APO. Promoted to *Generalleutnant* on 1 October 1943, on 1 October 1944 he took over the Army Personnel Office. One month later he achieved the rank of *General der Infanterie*. Burgdorf shot himself in Berlin on 2 May 1945.

Georg Eberhardt was born in Frankenhausen on 27 February 1914. As an *SS-Sturmbannführer* he commanded the SS Panzer-Grenadier Battalion Narva and was killed in action west of Izyum on 18 July 1943. He was awarded the Knight's Cross posthumously on 4 August 1943.

Maximilian Freiherr von Edelsheim was born in Berlin on 6 July 1897, and in August 1914 joined the military as an officer cadet. On 15 December 1915 he became a *Leutnant* in the 2nd Ulan Regiment. On 10 November 1938 the Baron was placed in command of the 1st Bicycle Battalion, and on 1 April 1939 was promoted to *Oberstleutnant*. On 29 September 1941 he was simultaneously promoted to *Oberst* and placed in command of the 22nd Cavalry Regiment. The 26th Panzer Regiment and 20th Panzer Brigade followed in 1942. Three months after taking over the 24th Panzer Division, on 1 March 1943 von Edelsheim was promoted to *Generalmajor*. Promoted to *Generalleutnant* on 1 March 1944, on 21 September he became commanding general of XXXXVIII Panzer Corps. Von Edelsheim was decorated with the Knight's Cross with Oak Leaves and Swords.

Rudolf Friedrich was born in Zwickau on 23 August 1889, and in the spring of 1909 began his military career as an officer cadet. On 24 August 1910 he achieved the rank of *Leutnant* in Field Artillery Regiment 12. After the First World War and the *Reichswehr*, Friedrich—promoted to *Oberst* on 1 April 1936—assumed command of Artillery Regiment 4 on 1 October 1936. On 1 October 1939 he took over Arko 114. Promoted to *Generalmajor* on 1 April 1940 and to *Generalleutnant* on 1 April 1941, on 23 September of that year he took command of the 62nd Infantry Division. There followed the 327th Infantry Division from 30 October 1942 to 9 August 1943, and Harko 317 from 24 November 1943 to 15 March 1944. Leading the 312th Division from 5 May 1944, on 28 July he assumed command of Harko 317. Friedrich was killed on the Eastern Front in 1945.

Paul Gallas was born in Alt-Rehfelde on 25 January 1885. He joined the military on 4 October 1904, and on 15 August 1918 was promoted to *Leutnant* in Ulan Regiment 10. After serving in the *Reichswehr*, on 1 November 1934 he joined the staff of the Munich Officer School. Gallas was promoted to *Oberst* on 1 April 1939, and on 2 October assumed command of Bicycle Replacement Battalion 7. On 31 July 1941 he commanded Field Post 247, and on 25 June 1942 became a regimental commander in the 281st Security Division. Gallas was transferred to the 207th Security Division in 1943. Decorated with the German Cross in Gold, Gallas was killed in Estonia on 18 September 1944. He was posthumously promoted to *Generalmajor* with an effective date of 1 September 1944.

Kurt von Gottberg was born in Preußisch Wilten on 11 February 1896. After graduation he joined the army and took part in the First World War from 1914, winning the Iron Crosses, First and Second Class. Discharged as an *Oberleutnant*, from 1919 to 1924 he was a member of the Erhard Brigade. He joined the NSDAP and the SS (No. 45,913) in 1932, and from 1937 to 1939 worked in the Race and Settlement Head Office. As an *SS-Oberführer* he led the land office in Prague. From 1 October 1940 until 21 July 1942 Gottberg was head of the requisitioning office in the SS Head Office. With promotion to *SS-Brigadeführer* and *Generalmajor der Polizei* he took over the post of SS and Police Commander "White Ruthenia," and on 24 March 1943 he became deputy to the Senior SS and Police Commander "Central Russia." On 15 July 1943 he was promoted to *SS-Gruppenführer* and *Generalleutnant der Polizei*. Nine days after assuming the position of Senior SS and Police Commander "Central Russia" on 21 June 1944, followed promotion to *SS-Obergruppenführer* and *General der Waffen-SS und Polizei*. On 20 July 1944 von Gottberg was awarded the Knight's Cross. Captured by the Allies, on 31 May 1945 he committed suicide in Flensburg.

Anton Grasser was born in Bossendorf on 3 November 1891. He served in Grenadier Regiment 109 as a one-year volunteer beginning 1 October 1913. In 1915 he was promoted to *Leutnant der Reserve*. After serving in the First World War he joined the Baden State Police, and in 1935 joined the *Wehrmacht*. Promoted to *Oberstleutnant* on 1 March 1938, he commanded I Battalion, Infantry Regiment 119 in the Polish Campaign. Grasser assumed command of the regiment in 1940 and was promoted to *Oberst* on 1 March 1941. On 4 February 1942 he became commander of the 25th Infantry Division, and on 1 April was promoted to *Generalmajor*. Promoted to *Generalleutnant* on 1 January 1943, on 15 November Grasser was named commander of LVI Panzer Corps, followed by XXVI Army Corps on 1 January 1944. Promoted to *General der Infanterie* on 1 May, on 3 July 1944 he was placed in command of Army Detachment Narva. In autumn 1944 Grasser was placed in command of the 11th Army. Decorated with the Knight's Cross with Oak Leaves, from 1951 – 1953 Grasser commanded Federal Border Police West.

Walter Hartmann was born in Mühlheim in the Ruhr on 23 July 1891, and on 1 October 1910 joined the military as an officer cadet. He became a *Leutnant* in Field Artillery Regiment 12 on 22 April 1912. After the First World War and a period in the *Reichswehr*, he assumed command of Artillery Regiment 24, having been promoted to *Oberst* on 1 June 1938. In February 1940 he was placed in charge of Arko 140, and on 15 July 1941 was severely wounded, losing a leg and an arm. He did not leave the army, however, but instead assumed command of the 407th Division on 1 May 1942, having been promoted to *Generalmajor* on 1 October 1941. On 10 September he was given command of the 390th Field Training Division. Then, on 1 February 1943 he was promoted to *Generalleutnant* and placed in command of the 87th Infantry Division. Placed in command of I Army Corps on 20 January 1944, on 1 May 1944 *General der Artillerie* Hartmann was placed in command of the I Mountain Corps. Decorated with the Knight's Cross with Oak Leaves and Swords, Hartmann commanded the VIII Army Corps from 1 September 1944 and the XXIV PV from 1 April 1945.

Gustav Hoehne was born in Kruschwitz on 17 February 1893. He joined the Imperial Army as an officer cadet on 27 March 1911, and on 18 August 1912 was made *Leutnant* in Infantry Regiment 150. After the First World War and service in the *Reichswehr*, *Oberst* Hoehne (1 March 1938) assumed command of Infantry Regiment 28 on 10 November 1938. Promoted to *Generalmajor* on 1 August 1940, on 25 October he was given command of the 8th Jäger Division (light infantry). Promoted to *Generalleutnant* on 1 August 1942, he commanded the Laux Corps from 28 November 1942 to 2 March 1943. On 1 May Hoehne was promoted to *General der Infanterie*, and from 20 July 1943 to 10 September 1944 was commanding general of VIII Army Corps. Command of the LXXXIX Panzer Corps followed on 1 December 1944. Decorated with the Knight's Cross with Oak Leaves, Hoehne died in Oberursel in 1951.

Erich Hofmann was born in Vienna on 30 September 1889. He joined the Imperial Army as an officer cadet on 18 September 1909, and in 1912 became a *Leutnant* in the 1st Tirol Kaiserjäger Regiment. After the war Hofmann served in the Federal Austrian Army, then on 1 April 1938 he was appointed 1st general staff officer of the XVIII Army Corps with the rank of *Oberst*. At the start of the Second World War he commanded III Battalion, Infantry Regiment 27, and in October 1939 assumed command of Infantry Regiment 352. Promoted to *Generalmajor* on 1 September 1941, on 31 December 1942 he took over the 207th Security Division. In 1943-44 *Generalleutnant* Hofmann (1 September 1943) was battle commander of

Narva and Lake Peipus. He led the 93rd Infantry Division from 20 June 1944, and on 27 July took over the 560th Volksgrenadier Division. He was decorated with the German Cross in Gold.

Friedrich Jeckeln was born in Homberg/Schwarzwald on 2 February 1895. A soldier in the First World War, he later served in a *Freikorps* and worked in various occupations. He joined the NSDAP in 1929 and became a member of the SS (No. 4,367). Jeckeln became a Reichstag deputy in 1932, and from August 1933 until April 1936 was head of *SS-Obergruppenabschnitt* Nordwest in Brunswick. Promoted to *SS-Obergruppenführer*, he subsequently commanded *SS-Oberabschnitt Mitte* until July 1940. Simultaneously Senior SS and Police Commander Center since 1938, from July 1940 to May 1941 he held the same position as Senior SS and Police Commander West in Dusseldorf. On 29 June 1941 he assumed the position of Senior SS and Police Commander Russia-South and Ukraine, and from November 1941 Jeckeln was Senior SS and Police Commander Russia-North and Ostland (Baltic States). From 1942 he commanded various battle groups—usually in the anti-partisan role. In 1944 the suffix "*und General der Waffen-SS*" was added to the alcoholic Jeckeln's title. He finally commanded the Silesia Corps and the V Mountain Corps. In 1946 he was sentenced to death by a Soviet military court in Riga and was hanged in the city's former ghetto.

Philipp Kleffel was born in Birkenfelde on 9 December 1887. He joined the military on 25 November 1905, and on 18 May 1907 was promoted to *Leutnant* in Ulan Regiment 4. After the First World War and service in the *Reichswehr*, on 1 April 1936 *Oberst* Kleffel (1 October 1935) took over Cavalry Regiment 14. From 15 February 1938 he was Senior Cavalry Officer 4, and on 1 June of the following year he was promoted to *Generalmajor*. For a short time Kleffel was chief-of-staff of the acting headquarters, XI Army Corps, and from 15 April 1940 he commanded the 1st Infantry Division. His promotion to *Generalleutnant* was announced on 1 June 1941, and six months later Kleffel was commanding L Army Corps. Promoted to *General der Kavallerie*, from the beginning of March to mid-September 1943 he commanded I Army Corps. He subsequently served in acting XI Army Corps and in a special staff of the OKH. From 4 July 1944 Kleffel commanded the XVI Army Corps. This was followed on 16 December 1944 by command of XXX Army Corps, and from 20 March 1945 the 25th Army. Kleffel was decorated with the Knight's Cross of the Iron Cross on 17 February 1942.

Rudolf Koch-Erpach was born in Munich on 9 April 1886. On 14 July 1904 he joined the military as an officer cadet, and on 8 March 1906 was named *Leutnant* in the 2nd Ulan Regiment. An officer in the First World War and the *Reichswehr*, as an *Oberst* (1 April 1932) he commanded the 3rd Cavalry Brigade from 1 April 1934. Promoted to *Generalmajor* (1 January 1935), on 13 May he assumed command of the 8th Division. After promotion to *Generalleutnant* on 1 April 1937, on 1 November 1940 he was placed in command of LX Army Corps with the rank of *General der Kavallerie*. From 1 April to 15 May 1941 he commanded XXXV Army Corps. The Liaison Headquarters Breslau followed from 15 July 1941 to 30 April 1942, and command of the acting VIII Army Corps. From 16 February to 11 April 1945 Koch-

Erpach was commanding general of LVI Panzer Corps (Silesia Corps). The final command held by the *General*, who had been decorated with the Knight's Cross, was the 1st Army.

Bernhard Langhorst was born in Diepholz on 13 December 1913. He initially served in the army, but in 1939 he transferred to the *SS-Totenkopf* Division and was a member of the 14th Company, *SS-Totenkopf* Infantry Regiment 1. After a reserve officer course and promotion to *SS-Untersturmführer* he was transferred to the 20th SS Waffen-Grenadier Division. There, following promotion to *SS-Hauptsturmführer der Reserve*, he ultimately commanded the 20th SS Anti-Tank Battalion. Langhorst was decorated with the Knight's Cross on 5 April 1945. He was mayor of Diepholz from 1961 to 1979 and died in the city of his birth on 8 July 1996.

Karl Sigismund Litzmann was already an *SA-Gruppenführer* in 1931, and two years later was promoted to *SA-Obergruppenführer*. With that party rank he commanded *SA-Gruppe Tannenberg*, which encompassed East Prussia and Danzig. In 1934 he commanded SA Obergruppe II in Stettin and was simultaneously head of the Supreme Board for Horse Breeding and Testing. At the end of 1937 he advanced to Reich Inspector of Riding and Driving Training in Berlin. He held that post until named General Commissar of Estonia. When this ended, he joined the *Waffen-SS* and in April 1945 commanded the 37th SS Reconnaissance Battalion as an *SS-Sturmbannführer*.

Hinrich Lohse was born in Mühlenbarbeck in 1896. In 1915 he became a soldier, but the next year he was wounded and discharged from military service. In 1921 he joined the NSDAP, and four years later became *Gauleiter* in Schleswig-Holstein. In 1928 Lohse became a deputy in the Prussian *Landtag*, and five years later a *Reichstag* deputy. In March 1933 he was named Senior President of Schleswig-Holstein. In November 1941, as an *SA-Obergruppenführer*, he was named Reich Commissar for the Ostland (Baltic States). In 1948 the Bielefeld Denazification Trial Court sentenced him to 10 years imprisonment and the loss of his assets. Lohse was released from prison in 1951 and died on 25 February 1964.

Berthold Maack was born in Altona on 24 March 1898. He volunteered for the army in 1915, and in 1917 became a *Leutnant der Reserve* in the 1st Guards Reserve Regiment. In 1919-20 he served in the *Freikorps*, after which he became a salesman. Maack joined the SA in 1930, and one year later the SS. He achieved the rank of *SS-Standartenführer* on 5 October 1932 and commanded SS-Abschnitt IV. He subsequently served as chief-of-staff of *SS-Gruppe-Südost* (Silesia), and from 22 October to 4 December 1934 in the Dacahau concentration camp. On the latter day Maack was promoted to *SS-Oberführer* and subsequently commanded the 39th SS *Standarte*. Promoted to *SS-Brigadeführer* on 13 September 1936, he initially commanded *SS-Abschnitt XXVI* and from 1938 *SS-Abschnitt XXV*. At the beginning of 1940 he was taken into the *Waffen-SS—SS-Standarte Germania*—with the rank of *SS-Obersturmführer*. He subsequently served as an *SS-Obersturmbannführer* (as of 9 November 1941) and commander of the SS Anti-Tank Battalion *Wiking*.

From 4 May 1942 to 21 June 1944 Maack (*SS-Standartenführer* on 20 April 1943) served in the 6th SS Mountain Division *Nord*. He attended a division commanders' course from 8 September to 7 October 1944, and on 26 January 1945 took over the 26th SS Waffen-Grenadier Division (Hungarian No. 2). After the death of *SS-Brigadeführer* Augsberger he was given command of the 20th SS Waffen-Grenadier Division (Estonian No. 1). On 20 April 1945, while in that post, he was promoted to *SS-Brigadeführer und General der Waffen-SS*. In the final days of the Second World War he also served as chief-of-staff of VIII Army Corps.

Hjalmar Mäe was born in Toal, Estonia, on 24 October 1901. He studied philosophy at the Universities of Berlin, Vienna, and Innsbruck, and law in the Universities of Graz and Vienna. He became a Doctor of Philosophy and a Doctor of Political Science. A politician in Estonia since 1929, in 1941 the Germans named him the first Land Director of the Estonian self-government. He lived in Austria after the war.

Paul Maitla was born in Surdago, in the Dorpat district of Estonia. As an officer in the Estonian Army, he was taken into the Red Army in July 1940. He entered German service in 1941, and on 30 January 1944 he was named *Freiwilligen-Hauptsturmführer*. On 23 August of that year Maitla was awarded the Knight's Cross. Initially used as commander of I Battalion, 45th SS Waffen-Grenadier Regiment, in 1945 he led the entire regiment on the Silesian front. In May 1945 Maitla was shot by the Red Army in Czechoslovakia.

Hans Mützelfeldt was born on 8 August 1916 and joined the *Schutzstaffel* with number 184,296. On 1 September 1942 he achieved the rank of an active *SS-Hauptsturmführer*, and as *SS-Sturmbannführer* became first general staff officer of the 20th SS Waffen-Grenadier Division (Estonian No. 1).

Harald Nugiseks was born in the Järvamaa district of Estonia on 22 October 1921. In early July 1941, while attending school in Paide, he was drafted by the Red Army. The next month Nugiseks joined a *Wehrmacht* unit as a volunteer, and on 2 October joined the 185th Estonian Security Battalion. His one-year commitment expired in December 1942 and he left the *Wehrmacht*. Then, in April 1943 he joined the Estonian Legion. On 15 May he went to the SS NCO School in Lauenburg, graduating four months later as an *SS-Unterscharführer*. Wounded on 28 October 1943, on 21 December Nugiseks was awarded the Wound Badge in Black and the Infantry Assault Badge. The Iron Cross, Second Class followed on 27 February 1944, and the Iron Cross, First Class on 7 March 1944 on the Narva Front. Just a few days later, on 9 April 1944, he was awarded the Knight's Cross. On 13 April Nugiseks became seriously ill and was sent to Meran (South Tyrol). He rejoined the division in Neuhammer at the end of October. From there he was sent to the SS Officer School in Neweklau from 5 January to mid-March 1945. Taken prisoner on 7 May 1945, in December he was sent to Siberia. Released on 10 November 1946, he was arrested again on 13 February 1947 and imprisoned until 17 September 1953. He initially stayed in Siberia and did not return to Estonia until 1958.

Alfons Rebane was born in Walk, Estonia, on 24 June 1908. After graduating in Narva he entered the officer school, graduating on 29 August 1928 with the rank of first-lieutenant. As a member of the Estonian 1st Armored Regiment he was promoted to lieutenant on 24 February 1933. At times attached to the Minister of Defense, following the annexation of the country by the Red Army in the summer of 1940 he was released from military service. On 1 September 1941 Rebane entered the service of the German military as commander of the 15th Company, 184th Security Group. Promoted to *Hauptmann* on 1 January 1942, in September he took over the Estonian Eastern Battalion 658. Promoted to *Major* in June 1943, he commanded the battalion at the Volkhov River and Novgorod. In February 1944 Rebane's unit was at the Narva River. Together with his men Rebane was taken into II Battalion, 47th SS Waffen-Grenadier Regiment. On 26 July 1944 he was named *Waffen-Sturmbannführer* and commander of the 46th SS Waffen-Grenadier Regiment. On 9 November that year he was promoted to *Waffen-Obersturmbannführer* and to *Waffen-Standartenführer* in March 1945. Rebane became the first Estonian to receive the Knight's Cross on 23 February 1944, and on 9 May 1945 he was awarded the Oak Leaves. He died in Augsburg, Germany, on 8 March 1976.

Emil Rehfeldt was born on 5 June 1907. He joined the SS and received membership number 337,331. On 9 November 1943 he achieved the rank of *SS-Obersturmbannführer*.

Haralt Riipalu was born in St. Petersburg on 13 February 1912. Promoted to *Waffen-Obersturmbannführer* on 28 July 1944, on 23 August he received the Knight's Cross as commander of the 45th SS Waffen-Grenadier Regiment. He died in England on 4 April 1960.

Franz von Roques was born in Treysa on 1 September 1977. He entered the military as an officer cadet on 28 February 1896, and on 20 July 1897 became a *Leutnant* in Infantry Regiment 81. After the First World War, on 1 April 1929 he became Inspector of Signals Troops in the *Reichswehr*. On 1 February 1931 he was promoted to *Generalmajor* and made infantry commander of VI Corps. Promoted to *Generalleutnant* on 1 January 1933, he was retired on 30 September. Reactivated, when the war started he was commander of the 177th Infantry Division. On account of his age, on 1 July 1940 von Roques was named General z.b.V.I. The following year he was commanding general of security troops and commander in Army Group North, and on 1 July 1941 was promoted to *General der Infanterie z.V.* His mobile employment was ended on 31 July 1943.

Edwin Count von Rothkirch und Trach was born in Militsch on 1 November 1888. He served as a *Leutnant* in Dragoon Regiment 17, and after the First World War and the *Reichswehr* commanded Cavalry Regiment 15. Promoted to *Oberst* on 1 April 1936, on 1 September 1939 Rothkirch was chief-of-staff of XXXIV Army Corps. Promoted to *Generalmajor* on 1 March 1940, at the end of April he took over the 442nd Reserve Division. From 11 October 1940 he commanded the 365th Military Government Area Headquarters (*Oberfeldkommandantur*), and from 5 January 1942 commanded the 330th Infantry Division. Two months later he was promoted to *Generalleutnant*. In September 1943 Rothkirch was named commander of Army Group Center's rear area, and then from 1 January 1944 he commanded various corps in an acting capacity. On 3 November 1944 he commanded LIII Army Corps.

Hando Ruus was born on 16 May 1917 in Reval and became a draftsman. He served in the 10th Infantry Battalion of the Estonian Army from 1 July 1938, achieving the rank of lieutenant. From 25 August to 13 September 1941 he served as a group leader in the Saku Self-Defense Force and afterwards in Police Battalion 38. On 28 October 1942 Ruus transferred to the Estonian Legion as an *SS-Untersturmführer*, and then fought at Cherkassy as a member of SS Panzer-Grenadier Battalion Narva. On 18 April 1944 he was named adjutant of the 20th SS Fusilier Battalion, and two days later was promoted to *SS-Obersturmführer*. Finally assuming command of the battalion, on 21-22 September 1944 Ruus was captured by the Soviets and was probably shot in 1945. Ruus was awarded the Iron Cross, First Class on 13 August 1943, and in his absence he was awarded the German Cross in Gold and promoted to *SS-Hauptsturmführer* on 30 December 1944.

Ferdinand Schörner was born in Munich on 12 June 1892, and on 1 October 1911 joined the Bavarian Lifeguard Regiment as a one-year volunteer. On 7 August 1914 he went to the field with the regiment as a *Vize-Feldwebel*, and on 29 November 1914 was named *Leutnant der Reserve*. An active officer since 1917, Schörner achieved the rank of *Oberstleutnant* 20 years later on 1 March 1937. In October of that year he took over Mountain Infantry Regiment 98. Promoted to *Generalmajor* on 1 August 1940 (*Oberst* since 27 August 1939), from 1 June 1940 he commanded the 6th Mountain Division. Schörner was named commanding general of XIX Mountain Corps on 15 January 1942. At the end of the month he was promoted to *Generalleutnant* and on 1 June 1942 to *General der Gebirgstruppen*. From 1 October 1943 to 1 February 1944 he commanded XXXX Panzer Corps and subsequently worked as head of the army's National-Socialist Operations Staff. He took over the 17th Army on 2 March 1944, and four weeks later Schörner was named *Generaloberst* and commander-in-chief of Army Group South. Decorated with the Knight's Cross with Oak Leaves, Swords and Diamonds, Schörner was promoted to *Generalfeldmarschall,* and in Hitler's will was named Commander-in-Chief of the Army. He returned from Soviet captivity in 1955.

Friedrich Schulz was born in Nettkow on 15 October 1897. He joined Field Artillery Regiment 54 as a wartime volunteer on 19 September 1914, and on 26 June 1916 was named *Leutnant* in the 58th Infantry Regiment. After the First World War and service in the *Reichswehr,* from 1 October 1937 Schulz served in the OKW's general staff. Promoted to *Oberstleutnant* on 1 February 1939, Schulz was in that same position when the war broke out. On 20 April 1940 he was chief-of-staff of XXXXIII Army Corps and was promoted to *Oberst* on 1 January of the following year. Schulz took over the same position in the 11th Army on 12 May 1942. Barely two months later he was promoted to *Generalmajor*. From 27 November 1942 to 1 March 1943 he headed the general staff of Army Group Don and South. After a division commander's course, on 1 May 1943 Schulz was given command of the

28th Jäger Division. He was promoted to *Generalleutnant* two months later. From 1 December 1943 he led III Panzer Corps for a month and from 8 February 1944 LIX Army Corps for six weeks. Schulz was promoted to *General der Infanterie* ten days after taking over the XXXXVI Panzer Corps on 22 March 1944. Decorated with the Knight's Cross with Oak Leaves and Swords, from 25 July 1944 the general commanded the 17th Army and finally Army Group South.

Johannes Soodla was born in Estonia on 14 January 1897. Promoted to colonel on 24 February 1940, he worked as commander of the Estonian military academy. When the Red Army entered the country in July 1940 Soodla fled to Germany. He returned to Estonia in 1941 after its conquest by the *Wehrmacht*, and in 1943 he and Juhan Tuuling became the only *Legion-Standartenführer* of the Estonian Legion. In August of that year he commanded the Legion's 1st Regiment. When Franz Augsberger assumed command, Soodla was named inspector-general of the Estonian Legion. He was promoted to *Legions-Oberführer*, and on 15 September 1944 to *Waffen-Brigadeführer und Generalmajor*. In spring 1944 he realized the formation of six Estonian Border Police Regiments. After the war he lived in West Germany, and from there fled to Florida. He later returned to West Germany and died in Goslar on 26 May 1965.

Dr. Walther Stahlecker was born in Sternenfels on 10 October 1900. He attended school in Königsberg, and in March 1914 was accepted as an officer cadet in the 5th East Prussian Infantry Regiment von Boyen No. 41 in Tilsit. Seriously wounded on the Eastern Front, on 27 January 1915 Steiner was awarded the Iron Cross, Second Class and the rank of *Leutnant*. In 1916 he was on the Courland Front and won the Iron Cross, First Class in the capture of Riga. After Russia's surrender he went to the Western Front, and in 1918 was discharged from the army in Danzig as an *Oberleutnant* and company commander. He served in an East Prussia *Freikorps* fighting against Lithuania, and on 1 October 1921 Steiner was taken into 8th Company, 1st Infantry Regiment in Tilsit as a platoon leader. In 1933 he was promoted to *Major* and left the *Reichswehr*. On 1 January 1935 Steiner became an advisor to the head of training and took over that post in August. With the introduction of compulsory military service in 1935 the post was dissolved, and on 12 June Steiner moved to the newly created *SS-Verfügungstruppe* with the rank of *SS-Sturmbannführer*. He was initially assigned to the *SS-Regiment Deutschland*. Tasked with formation of the *SS-Standarte Westland* on 1 August 1940, on 9 November Steiner was promoted to *SS-Brigadeführer und Generalmajor der Waffen-SS* and placed in command of the new *SS-Division Wiking*. Promoted to *SS-Gruppenführer und Generalleutnant der Waffen-SS* (1 January 1942), from November 1942 to January 1943 he commanded III Panzer Corps (Army) and in March 1943 began forming III (Germanic) Panzer Corps. On 1 July 1943 he was promoted to *SS-Obergruppenführer und General der Waffen-SS*. On 23 January 1945 Himmler made Steiner commander-in-chief of the 11th Panzer Army. The resulting discrepancies resulted in him being named commander of the special headquarters "Central Registration Organ of all *Wehrmacht* Elements in the Rear Area" from 23 February to 24 March 1945. In the final weeks of the war Steiner took over another frontline command; with the euphemistic title Army Detachment Steiner it was little more than a farce. Released from captivity on 27 April 1948, the *General*, who was decorated with the Knight's Cross with Oak Leaves and Swords, died in Munich on 12 May 1966.

Paul Vent initially commanded the 42nd SS Volunteer Grenadier Regiment as a *Freiwilligen-Sturmbannführer*. Promoted to *Freiwilligen-Obersturmbannführer*, he led the regiment, renamed the 45th SS Volunteer Grenadier Regiment, until April 1944. Finally, as a *Waffen-Standartenführer* he commanded the 47th SS Volunteer Grenadier Regiment. On the day of the Soviet major offensive in southern Estonia he lost his nerve and ran drunk to the Soviet lines, where he was captured by Red Army soldiers.

Herbert Wagner was born in Stuttgart on 19 January 1896. He joined the military as an officer cadet on 2 August 1914, and on 19 July 1915 made *Leutnant* with the 29th Field Artillery Regiment. He served in the *Reichswehr* after the First World War. Promoted to *Oberstleutnant* on 1 August 1937, one month later he became first general staff officer of I Army Corps. He held the same position with the 3rd Army when the Polish campaign began, and on 15 October was transferred to the army general staff. Wagner was promoted to *Oberst* on 1 February 1940, and on 6 December 1942 was given command of Infantry Regiment 215. On 30 March 1943 he took over Infantry Regiment 405. Before his promotion to *Generalmajor* on 1 August, on 30 June he became acting commander of the 212th Infantry Division. On 12 August 1943 he assumed command of the 132nd Infantry Division. Decorated with the Knight's Cross on 23 October 1944, on 8 January 1945 he took over Harko 302.

Jürgen Wagner was born in Strasbourg, Alsace, on 9 September 1901. He joined the Naumburg Cadet Corps in 1915, and in 1917 served in the Main Cadet Institute in Berlin-Lichterfelde. Wagner joined the *Reichswehr* in 1921, and in 1925 was named *Fahnenjunker*, but one year later he was discharged from the army. He joined the SS in March 1931. Promoted to *SS-Sturmbannführer* on 1 October 1933, he assumed command of II Battalion, *Leibstandarte der SS Adolf Hitler*. Wagner was promoted to *SS-Obersturmbannführer* on 4 July 1934. After employment in the headquarters of the *SS-Standarte Deutschland*, on 8 July 1943 he was named commander of the *SS-Regiment Der Führer*. On 1 September he assumed command of *SS-Infanterie-Regiment (mot.) 11*. Wagner later served with the *SS-Panzergrenadier-Division Wiking* as an *SS-Standartenführer* from 15 July 1942 and as *SS-Oberführer* from 9 November. Promoted to *SS-Brigadeführer und Generalmajor der Waffen-SS*, he took command of the *4. SS-Freiwilligen-Panzergrenadier-Brigade Nederland* in Croatia. Decorated with the Knight's Cross on 14 July 1943 and the Oak Leaves on 29 December 1944, in 1947 Wagner was hanged in Yugoslavia for his actions against partisans during formation of the brigade in 1943-44.

Appendix 5

Waffen-SS/Wehrmacht Ranks 1944

SS-Grenadier	Waffen-Grenadier[87]	Grenadier
SS-Sturmmann	Waffen-Sturmmann	Gefreiter
SS-Rottenführer	Waffen-Rottenführer	Obergefreiter
SS-Unterscharführer	Waffen-SS-Unterscharrführer	Unteroffizier
SS-Scharführer	Waffen-Scharführer	Unterfeldwebel
SS-Oberscharführer	Waffen-Oberscharführer	Feldwebel
SS-Hauptscharführer	Waffen-Hauptscharführer	Oberfeldwebel
SS-Untersturmführer	Waffen-Untersturmführer	Leutnant
SS-Obersturmführer	Waffen-Obersturmführer	Oberleutnant
SS-Hauptsturmführer	Waffen-Hauptsturmführer	Hauptmann
SS-Sturmbannführer	Waffen-Sturmbannführer	Major
SS-Obersturmbannführer	Waffen-Obersturmbannführer	Oberstleutnant
SS-Standartenführer	Waffen-Standartenführer	Oberst
SS-Oberführer	Waffen-Oberführer	no comparable rank
SS-Brigadeführer	Waffen-Brigadeführer	Generalmajor
SS-Gruppenführer	Waffen-Gruppenführer	Generalleutnant
SS-Obergruppenführer	Waffen-Obergruppenführer	General
SS-Oberstgruppenführer	Waffen-Oberstgruppenführer	Generaloberst

Endnotes

[1] Russia did not recognize this, however, until the Peace of Dorpat was signed on 2 February 1920.

[2] Stalin allowed his NKVD absolute free reign, especially during the last days of his influence in the summer of 1941. By the last day of fighting on 28 August 1941 (capture of Reval) the Red Army had mobilized 35,582 Estonians and taken away or killed 59,317 people.

[3] Also see Stephan Bandera and other Ukrainian nationalists. See: Michaelis, Rolf: Ukrainer in der Waffen-SS, Berlin 2000.

[4] See Appendix 4.

[5] See Appendix 4.

[6] This is also shown in a report by *Einsatzgruppe A*, according to which "only" 474 Jews and 684 communists were shot in Estonia by the end of October 1941, while in Lithuania the figures were 80,311 Jews and 860 communists, and in Latvia 30,025 Jews and 1,843 communists. In contrast to the numerous Latvians, Lithuanians, and Ukrainians, no Estonians served as concentration camp guards.

[7] See Appendix 4.

[8] See Appendix 4.

[9] The numbers 181 and following were created by combining the 18 from the 18th Army with a sequence of battalion numbers beginning at 1.

[10] The police of the former Estonian state were directed from a central headquarters as so-called State Police. In terms of personnel and materiel they were adequate for the tasks they faced at that time. Until the arrival of the Red Army their strength was approximately 1,700 men. The country was divided into 12 police prefectures corresponding to the existing administrative districts. Each prefecture was divided into 3 or 4 police commissariats, which in turn were divided into police districts. In the rural areas policing was the responsibility of police posts. When the Soviet Union assumed authority in 1940 the Estonian police were completely removed and replaced by a militia and a political police force. 70 to 80% of the former policemen were killed in a Soviet purge. Thus, when the German armed forces entered the country there was no usable police structure for them to fall back on.

[11] The police units (*Schutzmannschaften*) were initially supposed to be equipped exclusively with captured equipment. As the Red Army emptied or destroyed the clothing depots when it withdrew from the country, the volunteers could not be provided with standard uniforms. Gradually they received uniforms of the former Latvian armed forces and finally German police uniforms.

[12] Anti-partisan efforts were directed mainly against Soviet soldiers who had become separated from their units during combat operations in Estonia (until 21 October 1941) and hid out in the forests. Forming small groups, these were soon organized under a central command to carry out diversionary actions. In the course of the anti-partisan actions there

were also acts of brutality by the Estonian side, possibly spurred by a desire for revenge for the suffering in 1940-41.

[13] These were originally organized into police battalions for mobile anti-partisan warfare and (O) and (W) type police units for police-type order services and guard and security duties, respectively.

[14] On 14 May 1944 Himmler instituted the prefix "SS" for the Estonian border police regiments.

[15] From 15 March to 20 September 1944 3,000 Estonian children (ages 15 and up) were drafted as air force or navy auxiliaries.

[16] The division had been formed on 1 May 1944 from the headquarters of the destroyed 13th Luftwaffe Field Division and commanded the 2nd, 4th, 5th, and 6th Estonian SS Border Police Regiments. According to a report, 6 officers and 923 enlisted men deserted from the 4th and 6th Regiments alone by the end of July 1944—most felt abandoned by the Germans and had no desire to die in a hopeless struggle.

[17] See Appendix 4.

[18] See Appendix 4.

[19] Such units already existed at that time, for example made up of Danes, Finns, Flemings, Dutch, or Norwegians.

[20] SS-FHA, Diary No. 5960/42 secret command matter of 29 September 1942.

[21] See Appendix 4.

[22] Among them *SS-Untersturmführer* Schmidt and *SS-Untersturmführer* Langhorst.

[23] See Appendix 4.

[24] The members of the SS Panzer-Grenadier Battalion Narva were issued the SS collar patch before going into action. In Estonia some units then fabricated collar patches with the medallion of the Estonian freedom cross. Finally, in summer 1944 the SS-FHA issued patches made in Germany, with a sword to the right of the "E." This was not accepted by the units, however, and so the SS-FHA finally accepted the Estonian-made insignia and took over its production.

[25] See Appendix 4.

[26] SS-FHA, Diary No. 8699/42 secret command matter of 21 January 1943. The company had previously been deployed in the Reichkommissariat Ostland, where it participated in numerous mass shootings of Jews. For example, on 11 May 1942 the company reported shooting 1,000 Jews near Minsk, another 1,000 Jews near Minsk on 15 June 1942, the liquidation of 4,000 Jews near Slonim on 27 June 1942, and the killing of another 6,000 Jews in Minsk on 28 July 1942.

[27] SS-FHA, Diary No. II/2753/43 secret command matter of 17 April 1943. It initially consisted of 4 officers, 7 NCOs, and 6 enlisted men as German core personnel and 3 Estonian officers, 17 NCOs, and 79 enlisted men.

[28] See Appendix 4.

[29] SS-FHA, Diary No. II/208/43 secret command matter of 23 March 1943. The battalion consisted of 15 German officers, 56 NCOs, and 128 enlisted men plus 7 Estonian officers, 68 NCOs, and 701 enlisted men.

[30] On Saturday, 17 July 1943, after the failure of the German "Operation Citadel" at Kursk, the Soviet Southwest Front (Army General Malinovsky) and the South Front (Colonel-General Tolbuchin) launched a counterattack at the Donets, near Izyum, and on the Mius, shaking the entire Eastern Front.

[31] Under the corps' command were: 5th SS Panzer-Grenadier Division Wiking, *SS Sturmbrigade Wallonie*, and the 57th, 72nd, 167th, and 389th Infantry Divisions.

[32] Under the corps' command were: the 252nd, 106th, and 320th Infantry Divisions, plus the 8th SS Cavalry Division, 3rd and 11th Panzer Divisions, 10th Infantry Division, 14th Panzer Division, and the 376th Infantry Division.

[33] Encircled were: 5th, 72nd, 88th, 389th, 112th, 255th, and 332nd Infantry Divisions, plus the 5th SS Panzer-Grenadier Division Wiking and the SS Volunteer Assault Brigade *Wallonie*.

[34] SS-FHA, Diary No. II/211/43 secret command matter of 23 March 1943.

[35] The 1st SS Infantry Brigade (Mot.) had been formed in the General Government effective 24 April 1941, and three months later subordinated to the Senior SS and Police Commander South. Deployed in the greater Ostrog area, members of the brigade liquidated almost 5,000 Jews and suspected partisans in a few weeks. Developments at the front resulted in front-line action at Orel from early December 1941 to August 1942. After three and a half months of anti-partisan operations in White Russia, the brigade saw further action at the front from 1 December 1942 to 2 July 1943, this time at Velikiye Luki. In fact, however, the 1st SS Infantry Brigade was not reorganized into the Estonian SS Volunteer Brigade and renamed; rather, in January 1944 it formed the basis of the new 18th SS Volunteer Panzer-Grenadier Division Horst Wessel.

[36] SS-FHA, Diary No. 600/43 secret command matter of 5 May 1943.

[37] The battle group consisted of Police Regiments 9, 16, and 26, the Latvian Police Regiment Riga, the Latvian Police Battalions 313 and 316, the Estonian Police Battalion 286, and Police Signals Company 307.

[38] See Appendix 4.

[39] See Appendix 4.

[40] See Appendix 4.

[41] See Appendix 4.

[42] On Friday, 1 October 1943, the Soviet Kalinin Front (Army General Eremenko) advanced into the seam between the 16th Army and the 3rd Panzer Army in the direction of Nevel, Vitebsk, and Orsha. One week later the 3rd Shock Army (Lieutenant-General Giarasimov) took Nevel, while other units of the Red Army advanced on Polotsk and Vitebsk. Headquarters, 16th Army immediately ordered Nevel retaken. The 58th Infantry Division attacked on 8 October, but was driven back to its starting position. The gap between Army Groups North (16th Army) and Center (3rd Panzer Army) created by the Soviet breakthrough could not be closed. The army group headquarters therefore requested the *Wehrmacht* Commander of *Ostland* (*General der Kavallerie* Braemer) to defend the former Latvian border to the east. All available police and anti-partisan detachments were assembled under

the command of *SS-Obergruppenführer und General der Polizei* von dem Bach and inserted into the gap. As a result "Operation Heinrich" was cancelled and the units sent into the breakthrough area at Nevel.

[43] Lake Nesherda runs from north to south. It is approximately 12 km long and in places is two km wide. To its south is Lake Meshno, into which the Drissa River flows. This formed the boundary between Army Groups North and Center.

[44] This extended from the left wing of VIII Army Corps and Novosokolniki.

[45] See Appendix 4.

[46] After the heavy defensive fighting the commander-in-chief of the 16th Army, *General der Artillerie* Hansen, ordered I and XXXXIII Army Corps to pull back under the codename Case Green. I Army Corps reached the new area—on the right of VIII Army Corps to northeast of Polotsk to Army Group Center—on 5 January 1944.

[47] SS-FHA, Diary No. 180/44 secret command matter of 24 January 1944.

[48] At the end of March 1944 the 33rd SS Grenadier Training and Replacement Battalion moved from Heidelager to Klooga, near Reval.

[49] In the course of the general mobilization, on 14 February 1944 SS Replacement Detachment Estonia was formed from the *Waffen-SS* Replacement Detachment Ostland in 11 defense district sections: Reval, Hapsal, Arensburg, Pernau, Fellin, Dorpat, Werro, Weissenstein, Petschau, Walk, and Wesenburg, plus the SS Replacement Section Latvia in 7 defense district sections: Riga City, Riga Country, Libau, Mitau, Wolmar, Dvinsk (Dünaburg), and Rositten.

[50] Sworn statement of 10 June 1948 before the International Military Tribunal in Nuremberg.

[51] Hitler did not, however, grant the promised sovereignty of Estonia.

[52] See Appendix 4.

[53] See Appendix 4.

[54] The 207th Security Division had previously been deployed in the Narva sector, and after the defensive positions were taken over by III (Germanic) SS Panzer Corps on 3 February 1944 it was sent to Dorpat and tasked with defending the Lake Peipus narrows near Mehikoorma. In addition to its defensive tasks, the division headquarters was also to assume responsibility for equipping the border police regiments formed as a result of the Estonian mobilization.

[55] See Appendix 4.

[56] In January 1944 the Soviet forces received orders to destroy the 18th Army, liberate Leningrad, and reach the line Narva—Pskov—Velikaya, in order to create a base from which to conquer the Baltic States. On 14 January 1944 the Soviet 2nd Shock Army stormed out of the Oranienbaum bridgehead against the positions of the III (Germanic) SS Panzer Corps. The attack shattered the SS corps, which fell back toward the Narva in heavy fighting. The corps entered the Narva bridgehead at the end of January. On 4 February 1944 the elements of the 18th Army deployed north of Lake Peipus (III SS Panzer Corps and XXVI Army Corps) were combined into Army Group Narva (*General der Infanterie* Frießner). At the beginning of February II SS Panzer Corps, whose southern boundary ran just south of the city of Narva, had

to fight off further heavy attacks by the Soviet 47th Army, 2nd Shock Army, and 8th Army, and on 12 February 1944 was reinforced by the 20th Estonian SS Volunteer Division.

[57] Both former *Luftwaffe* field divisions had been largely destroyed in the Oranienbaum pocket and were disbanded at the beginning of February.

[58] See Appendix 4.

[59] Similarly the regiments were renamed *Waffen-Regimenter der SS*. The Estonian designation was *20. SS-Relvagrenaderide Diviis (Eesti Esimene)*.

[60] The Soviet 8th Army (Major-General Sukhomlin) crossed the river south of Narva, near Kriivasao, and overran elements of the 227th and 170th Infantry Divisions with the objective of reaching the coast, and thus encircling the III (Germanic) SS Panzer Corps. The bridgehead ran north of the mouth of the Piata into the Narva south of Auvere, and after about 16 km veered south through the Lanika Swamp to Omati and from there back toward the east bank of the Narva.

[61] *Waffen-Standartenführer* Tuuling was subsequently relieved of command of the regiment and *Waffen-Obersturmbannführer* Rebane was made regimental commander. Leo Sipelgas recalled:"*Waffen-Standartenführer Juhan Tuuling was a weak personality—he was no frontline officer. He died in Denmark in 1949. Rebane was a fighter, just like Riipalu and Maitla.*"

[62] Until then the division had been under the direct command of the 18th Army.

[63] This refers to the few combat-capable Estonian SS Border Police Regiments.

[64] III Battalion, 45th SS Waffen-Grenadier Regiment had been established in Klooga and Kehra from I and II Battalions, 20th SS Waffen-Grenadier/Training and Replacement Regiment using mobilized personnel with no training. For this reason half of the men were sent home before the unit saw its first action in the Tartu area. III Battalion, 47th SS Waffen-Grenadier Regiment was formed in Paldiski from III Battalion, 20th SS Waffen-Grenadier Training and Replacement Regiment, and on 22 July 1944 it marched into the Tannenberg Position. After the first battles the battalion's strength was reduced to just two companies.

[65] On 2 September 1944, after the heavy fighting at the Emajogi, battalion commander *Waffen-Hauptsturmführer* Pälin and 43 men were awarded the Iron Cross.

[66] I Battalion, 46th SS Waffen-Grenadier Regiment and II Battalion, 45th SS Waffen-Grenadier Regiment were still in the area of the Tannenberg Position. III Battalion, SS Waffen-Grenadier Regiment was attached to the 87th Infantry Division.

[67] Augsberger had flown to Berlin for a meeting on 6 September 1944.

[68] See Appendix 4.

[69] For example, Dr. Falta, the 11th SS Armored Reconnaissance Battalion's medical officer, was shot by an Estonian who obviously had no further interest in serving with the Germans.

[70] The 11th, 21st, 30th, 31st, and 218th Infantry Divisions, plus the 11th SS Volunteer Panzer-Grenadier Division Nordland and 4th SS Volunteer Panzer-Grenadier Brigade Nederland were subsequently transported to Courland.

[71] SS-FHA, diary No. 3572/44 secret command matter of 6 October 1944.

[72] Report by Headquarters Rothkirch, Ops Officer Diary No. 4319/44 of 7 October 1944.
[73] Strength was 20 Estonian officers and 260 NCOs and enlisted men, plus 8 German officers and 20 NCOs and enlisted men.

[74] Strength: approximately 500 men.

[75] The main explanation for this is that the men had scarcely recovered from wounds and were poorly armed. There were no heavy weapons for use against tanks or aircraft—and it was impossible to fight such a battle with carbines.

[76] See Appendix 4.

[77] This line was held until mid-March 1945.

[78] Attachment of Battle Group Hofmann ended on 28 February 1945.

[79] At that time SS Battle Group Rehfeldt was still attached to Corps Detachment Friedrich.

[80] A comparison with the authorized equipment of an infantry division according to the 1944 table of organization shows that because of numerous secondments to army units the unit was almost at authorized strength—at least in heavy weapons:

Authorized Strength—Armament

rifles	8,598	K 43 automatic rifles	309
sniper rifles	513	anti-tank rocket launchers	108
pistols	2,013	submachine-guns	1,595
light machine-guns	614	heavy machine-guns	102
light mortars 81.4 mm	54	heavy mortars 120 mm	32
20 mm light anti-aircraft guns	13	flamethrowers	22
50 mm anti-tank guns	1	75 mm anti-tank guns	22
75 mm light infantry guns	19	150 mm heavy infantry guns	6
105 mm light howitzers	34	150 mm heavy howitzers	9
flare pistols	389	rifle grenade launchers	489

[81] See Appendix 4.

[82] This consisted of the 20th SS Anti-Tank Battalion, the workshop company, pioneers, and the 20th SS Waffen-Artillery Regiment. SS Battle Group Langhorst fought northeast of Ziegenhals from 19 to 23 March 1945. The next day it was disbanded and its component units transferred into the Schweidnik—Freiburg area.

[83] See Appendix 4.

[84] Further proof of the opinion held of the division with respect to the Oppeln Pocket is shown in the awarding of the Knight's Cross to *SS-Brigadeführer* Augsberger and *SS-Hauptsturmführer* Langhorst on 31 March and 5 April 1945, respectively.

[85] See Appendix 4.

[86] This was in keeping with Himmler's wish that every graduate from an officer school should serve as a platoon commander in the SS-Verfügungstruppe for 10 months, followed by 10 months in the Central Office for Race and Resettlement for ideological training. Usually the officer then had to serve 10 months in the SD as well. Following this the man was assigned to a unit or to one of the numerous SS offices.

[87] As of June 1944, the rank designations of foreign soldiers serving in armed units of the SS included the prefix "Waffen" instead of "SS" or "Freiwilliger."

Bibliography

Birm, Ruth: Die Höheren SS- und Polizeiführer, Tübingen 1985

Dallin, Alexander: Deutsche Herrschaft in Rußland, Düsseldorf 1958

Friessner, Hans: Verratene Schlachten, Hamburg 1956

Haupt, Wemer: Die Heeresgruppe Mitte, Bad Nauheim 1966

Heiber, Helmut (Hrsg.): Lagebesprechungen im Führerhauptquartier, Milnchen 1964

Jurs, August (Hrsg.): Estonian Freedomfighters in the World War Two, o. O., o. J.

Keilig, Wolfe: Die Generale der Heers, Bad Nauheim 1983

Klietmann, Dr. K.-G.: Die Waffen-SS, Osnabrück 1965

Krätschmer, Ernst-Günther: Die Ritterkreuzträger der Waffen-SS, Pr. Oldendorf 1982

Michaelis, Rolf: Die Grenadier-Divisionen der Waffen-SS (I-III), Erlangen 1994/95

Müller, G., Guthmann, F. W.: Die Geschichte der 207. und 281. Infanterie-Division, Dortmund 1958

Neulen, Hans Wemer: An deutscher Seite, München 1985

Preradovich, Nikolaus von: Die Generale der Waffen-SS, Berg 1985

Rürup, Reinhard (Hrsg.): Der Krieg gegen die Sowjetunion 1941-1945, Berlin 1991^2

Taylor, Huge Page: Uniforms, Organization And History Of The Waffen-SS (Bd. 5), San Jose 1986^2

Register of Names

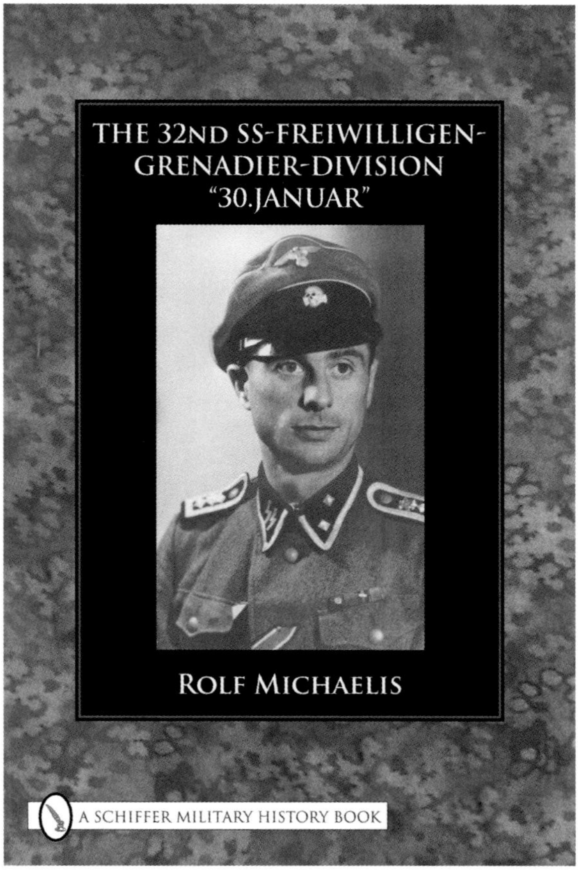

The 32nd SS-Freiwilligen-Grenadier-Division: "30.Januar". Rolf Michaelis. The SS Division "30. Januar" was one of the last SS-Divisions formed during World War II and was almost entirely composed of training units and 16-18 year old boys (the honorary name "30. Januar" was the same date Hitler became Reich chancellor in 1933). First planned as a motorized division, the unit ended up as a normal infantry division because of a lack of fuel. With a final strength of 12,000, they fought on the Oder-front south of Frankfurt/Oder. After the Soviet attack on 16 April 1945 they were wiped out in the pocket of Halbe southeast of Berlin.
Size: 6" x 9" • over 80 bw images • 128 pp.
ISBN: 978-0-7643-3101-5 • hard cover • 35.00

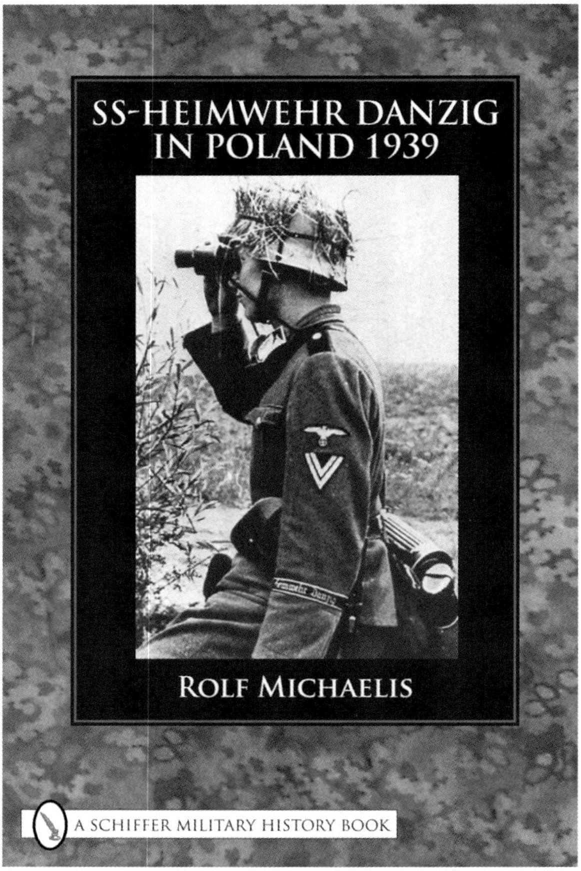
SS-HEIMWEHR DANZIG
IN POLAND 1939
ROLF MICHAELIS
A SCHIFFER MILITARY HISTORY BOOK

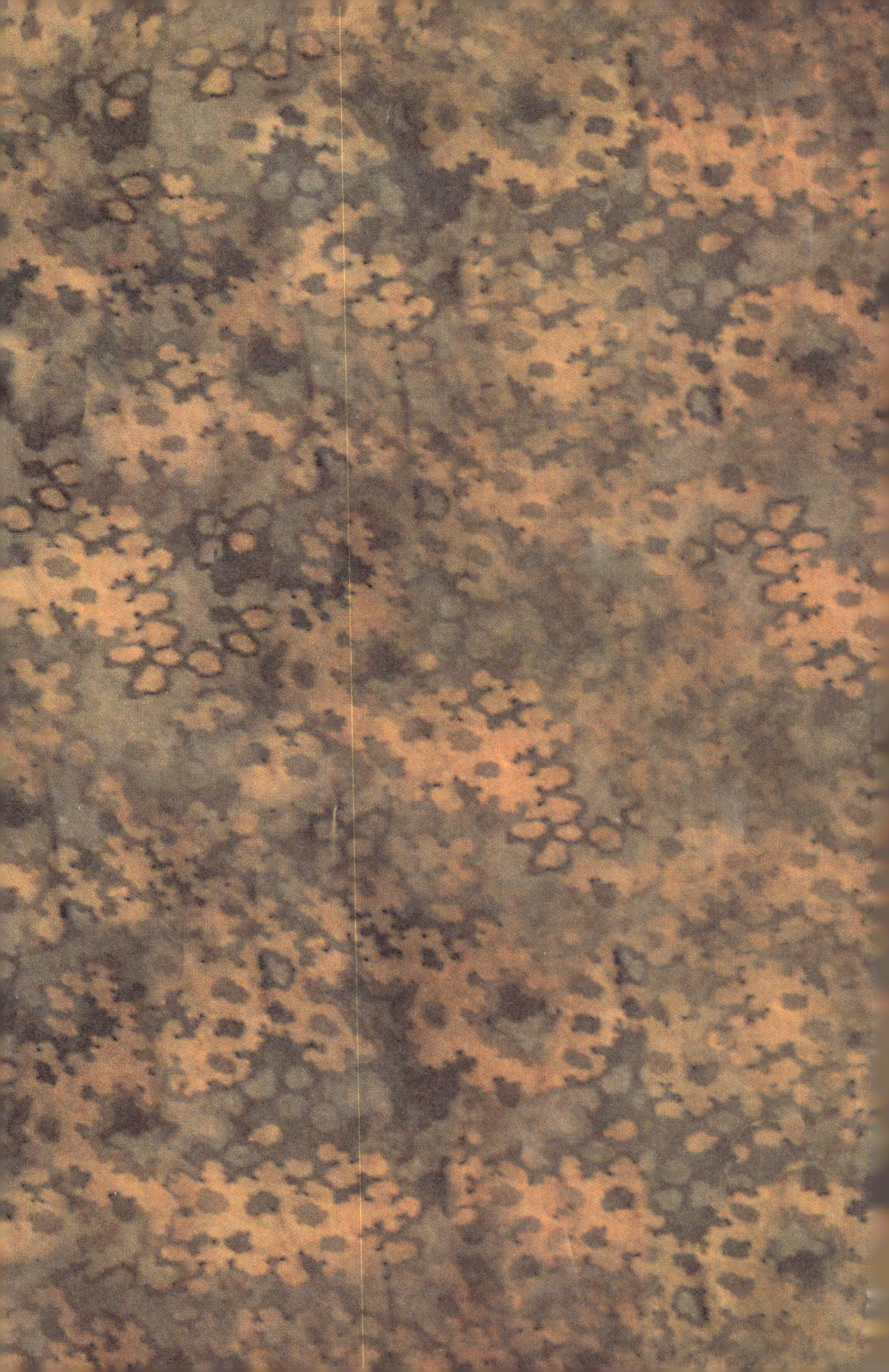